T0273091

Birds of
Texas
Field Guide

Stan Tekiela

Adventure Publications
Cambridge, Minnesota

Dedication

To my wife, Katherine, and daughter, Abigail, with all my love

Acknowledgments

Special thanks to the National Wildlife Refuge System, which stewards the land that is critical to many bird species. Special thanks also to David Sarkozíorida for reviewing the range maps.

Edited by Sandy Livoti and Dan Downing

Cover, book design and illustrations by Jonathan Norberg

Range maps produced by Anthony Hertzel

Cover photo: Painted Bunting by Stan Tekiela
All photos by Stan Tekiela except pp. 78, 434 (male) by **Agami Photo Agency/Shutterstock**; p. 278 (juvenile) by **Albert Barr/Shutterstock**; pp. 58 (non-breeding), 170, 266 (all), 374, 376, 394 (juvenile), 416 (female) and 430 by **Rick and Nora Bowers**; pp. 24 (Bronzed Cowbird), 210 (displaying), 254 (juvenile), 272 (juvenile and chick-feeding adult) and 332 (displaying) by **Dudley Edmondson**; pp. 50 (soaring) and 398 (winter) by **Kevin T. Karlson**; pp. 162 and 342 (in flight) by **Brian E Kushner/ Shutterstock**; p. 50 (drying) by **JayPierstorff/Shutterstock**; p. 174 (breeding) by **Paul Reeves Photography/Shutterstock**; pp. 398 (main and in flight) and 434 (female) by **Brian E. Small**; p. 112 (female) by **Sundry Photography/Shutterstock**; p. 316 (displaying) by **Hartmut Walter**; pp. 50 (juvenile), 52 (juvenile), 188 (both juveniles), 268 (juvenile), 334 (juvenile) and 336 (in-flight juvenile) by **Brian K. Wheeler**; and pp. 250, 324 (main) and 418 (female) by **Jim Zipp**

To the best of the publisher's knowledge, all photos were of live birds. Some were photographed in a controlled condition.

15 14 13 12 11 10 9 8

Birds of Texas Field Guide
First Edition 2004
Second Edition 2020
Copyright © 2004 and 2020 by Stan Tekiela
Published by Adventure Publications
An imprint of AdventureKEEN
310 Garfield Street South
Cambridge, Minnesota 55008
(800) 678-7006
www.adventurepublications.net
ISBN 978-1-64755-062-2 (pbk.); 978-1-64755-063-9 (ebook)

TABLE OF CONTENTS

WHAT'S NEW?

It is hard to believe that it's been more than 15 years since the debut of *Birds of Texas Field Guide*. This critically acclaimed field guide has helped countless people identify and enjoy the birds that we love. Now, in this expanded third edition, *Birds of Texas Field Guide* has many new and exciting changes and a fresh look, while retaining the same familiar, easy-to-use format.

To help you identify even more birds in Texas, I have added 7 new species and more than 150 new color photographs. All of the range maps have been meticulously reviewed, and many updates have been made to reflect the ever-changing movements of the birds.

Everyone's favorite section, "Stan's Notes," has been expanded to include even more natural history information. "Compare" sections have been updated to help ensure that you correctly identify your bird, and additional feeder information has been added to help with bird feeding. I hope you will enjoy this great new edition as you continue to learn about and appreciate our Texas birds!

WHY WATCH BIRDS IN TEXAS?

Millions of people have discovered bird feeding. It's a simple and enjoyable way to bring the beauty of birds closer to your home. Watching birds at your feeder often leads to a lifetime pursuit of bird identification. The *Birds of Texas Field Guide* is for those who want to identify the common birds of Texas.

There are over 1,100 bird species in North America. In Texas alone there have been more than 500 different kinds of birds recorded throughout the years. These bird sightings were documented by hundreds of bird watchers and became a part of the official state record. From these valuable records, I've chosen 176 of the most common birds of Texas to include in this field guide.

Bird watching, or birding, is one of the most popular activities in America. Its appeal in Texas is due, in part, to an unusually rich and abundant birdlife. Why are there so many birds? One of the reasons is open space. Texas is the second-largest state, with over 268,500 square miles (695,400 sq. km) and about 29 million people. On average, that is only 96 people per square mile (30 per sq. km).

Open space is not the only reason there is such an abundance of birds. It is also the diversity of habitat. Texas can be broken into four distinctive physiographic provinces or habitats–Coastal Plain, Central Lowland, Great Plains and the Basin and Range Province–each of which supports a different group of birds.

The Coastal Plain makes up most of eastern and southern Texas, a full one-third of the state. The region near the coast is flat and low-lying. There are 367 miles (591 km) of coastline along the Gulf of Mexico, with a total of 3,359 miles (5,408 km) of coast including the inlets and islands. The Coastal Plain is a great place to see hundreds of birds such as American White Pelicans and Caspian Terns.

The Central Lowland and Great Plains regions occupy much of central and northern Texas. This wide, expansive area with a few eroded river valleys is known for its large ranches and cattle grazing. It has a semiarid climate and is a great place to see the Roadrunner and Golden Eagle.

The Basin and Range Province lies to the west of the Great Plains in western Texas. This region has some of the finest scenery in the state and several mountain ranges, including Guadalupe Mountains and Guadalupe Peak. Reaching an elevation of 8,749 feet (2,650 m) above sea level, it is the highest point in Texas. Here is a good place to see birds such as the Woodhouse's Scrub-Jay.

Water also plays a big part in the bird populations of Texas. The Rio Grande Valley stretches along the Rio Grande River and makes up a 1,000-mile (1,610 km) border with Mexico. The Rio Grande carries little water during most of the year, but will flood after periods of heavy rain. This area is one of the best places in Texas to see birds. Its warm climate and water sources are great places for many wonderful birds such as the Green Jay and Plain Chachalaca.

Damming the rivers has resulted in the formation of large reservoirs in Texas. The largest natural lake in the state is Caddo Lake, which is along the Louisiana border. It is not a single open body of water, but rather a winding network of channels. Several large artificial lakes include Lake Texoma on the Red River, Toledo Bend Reservoir on the Sabine River and Sam Rayburn Reservoir on a tributary of the Neches River. All of these lakes are good places to look for birds such as Blue-winged Teals and gulls.

Varying habitats in Texas also mean variations in the weather. Northern parts of Texas are cooler and moister than southern Texas. In fact, winters can be very cold in north central Texas.

Southern Texas can be warm even during winter, and coastal Texas is very moderate by comparison. Western Texas can be very hot and dry during summer and cold in winter.

No matter if you're in the hot, arid deserts or in the cool, moist mountains of Texas, there are birds to watch in each season. Whether witnessing hawks migrating in autumn or welcoming back hummingbirds in spring, there is variety and excitement in birding as each season turns to the next.

OBSERVE WITH A STRATEGY: TIPS FOR IDENTIFYING BIRDS

Identifying birds isn't as difficult as you might think. By simply following a few basic strategies, you can increase your chances of successfully identifying most birds that you see. One of the first and easiest things to do when you see a new bird is to note its **color**. This field guide is organized by color, so simply turn to the right color section to find it.

Next, note the **size of the bird.** A strategy to quickly estimate size is to compare different birds. Pick a small, a medium and a large bird. Select an American Robin as the medium bird. Measured from bill tip to tail tip, a robin is 10 inches (25 cm). Now select two other birds, one smaller and one larger. Good choices are a House Sparrow, at about 6 inches (15 cm), and an American Crow, around 18 inches (45 cm). When you see a species you don't know, you can now quickly ask yourself, "Is it larger than a sparrow but smaller than a robin?" When you look in your field guide to identify your bird, you would check the species that are roughly 6–10 inches (15–25 cm). This will help to narrow your choices.

Next, note the **size, shape and color of the bill.** Is it long or short, thick or thin, pointed or blunt, curved or straight? Seed-eating birds, such as Blue Grosbeaks, have bills that are thick and strong enough to crack even the toughest seeds. Birds that sip nectar, such as Black-chinned Hummingbirds, need long, thin bills to reach deep into flowers. Hawks and owls tear their prey with very sharp, curving bills. Sometimes, just noting the bill shape can help you decide whether the bird is a woodpecker, finch, grosbeak, blackbird or bird of prey.

Next, take a look around and note the **habitat** in which you see the bird. Is it wading in a saltwater marsh? Walking along a riverbank or on the beach? Soaring in the sky? Is it perched high in the trees or hopping along the forest floor? Because of diet and habitat preferences, you'll often see robins hopping on the ground but not usually eating seeds at a feeder. Or you'll see a Blue Jay sitting on a tree branch but not climbing headfirst down the trunk, like a Red-headed Nuthatch would.

Noticing **what the bird is eating** will give you another clue to help you identify the species. Feeding is a big part of any bird's life. Fully one-third of all bird activity revolves around searching for food, catching prey and eating. While birds don't always follow all the rules of their diet, you can make some general assumptions. Northern Flickers, for instance, feed on ants and other insects, so you wouldn't expect to see them visiting a seed feeder. Other birds, such as Barn and Cliff Swallows, eat flying insects and spend hours swooping and diving to catch a meal.

Sometimes you can identify a bird by **the way it perches.** Body posture can help you differentiate between an American Crow and a Red-tailed Hawk, for example. Crows lean forward over their feet on a branch, while hawks perch in a vertical position. Consider posture the next time you see an unidentified large bird in a tree.

Birds in flight are harder to identify, but noting the **wing size and shape** will help. Wing size is in direct proportion to body size, weight and type of flight. Wing shape determines whether the bird flies fast and with precision, or slowly and less precisely. Barn Swallows, for instance, have short, pointed wings that slice through the air, enabling swift, accurate flight. Turkey Vultures have long, broad wings for soaring on warm updrafts. House Finches have short, rounded wings, helping them to flit through thick tangles of branches.

Some bird species have a unique **pattern of flight** that can help in identification. American Goldfinches fly in a distinctive undulating pattern that makes it look like they're riding a roller coaster.

While it's not easy to make all of these observations in the short time you often have to watch a "mystery" bird, practicing these identification methods will greatly expand your birding skills. To further improve your skills, seek the guidance of a more experienced birder who can answer your questions on the spot.

BIRD BASICS

It's easier to identify birds and communicate about them if you know the names of the different parts of a bird. For instance, it's more effective to use the word "crest" to indicate the set of extra-long feathers on top of a Northern Cardinal's head than to try to describe it.

The following illustration points out the basic parts of a bird. Because it is a composite of many birds, it shouldn't be confused with any actual bird.

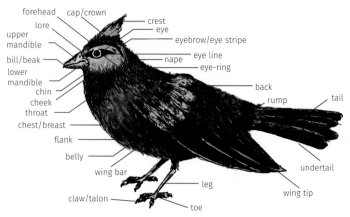

Bird Color Variables

No other animal has a color palette like a bird's. Brilliant blues, lemon yellows, showy reds and iridescent greens are common in the bird world. In general, male birds are more colorful than their female counterparts. This helps males attract a mate, essentially saying, "Hey, look at me!" Color calls attention to a male's health as well. The better the condition of his feathers, the better his food source, territory and potential for mating.

Male and female birds that don't look like each other are called sexually dimorphic, meaning "two forms." Dimorphic females often have a nondescript dull color, as seen in Indigo Buntings. Muted tones help females hide during the weeks of motionless incubation and draw less attention to them when they're out feeding or taking a break from the rigors of raising the young.

The males of some species, such as the Downy Woodpecker, Blue Jay and Bald Eagle, look nearly identical to the females. In woodpeckers, the sexes are differentiated by only a red mark, or sometimes a yellow mark. Depending on the species, the mark may be on top of the head, on the face or nape of neck, or just behind the bill.

During the first year, juvenile birds often look like their mothers. Since brightly colored feathers are used mainly for attracting a mate, young non-breeding males don't have a need for colorful plumage. It's not until the first spring molt (or several years later, depending on the species) that young males obtain their breeding colors.

Both breeding and winter plumages are the result of molting. Molting is the process of dropping old, worn feathers and replacing them with new ones. All birds molt, typically twice a year, with the spring molt usually occurring in late winter. At this time, most birds produce their brighter breeding plumage, which lasts throughout the summer.

Winter plumage is the result of the late summer molt, which serves a couple of important functions. First, it adds feathers for warmth in the coming winter season. Second, in some species it produces feathers that tend to be drab in color, which helps to camouflage the birds and hide them from predators. The winter plumage of the male American Goldfinch, for example, is olive-brown, unlike its canary-yellow breeding color during summer. Luckily for us, some birds, such as the male Northern Cardinal, retain their bright summer colors all year long.

Bird Nests

Bird nests are a true feat of engineering. Imagine constructing a home that's strong enough to weather storms, large enough to hold your entire family, insulated enough to shelter them from cold and heat, and waterproof enough to keep out rain. Think about building it without blueprints or directions and using mainly your feet. Birds do this!

Before building, birds must select an appropriate site. In some species, such as the House Wren, the male picks out several potential sites and assembles small twigs in each. The "extra" nests, called dummy nests, discourage other birds from using any nearby cavities for their nests. The male takes the female around and shows her the choices. After choosing her favorite, she finishes the construction.

In other species, such as the Bullock's Oriole, the female selects the site and builds the nest, while the male offers an occasional suggestion. Each bird species has its own nest-building routine that is strictly followed.

As you can see in these illustrations, birds build a wide variety of nest types.

| ground nest | platform nest | cup nest | pendulous nest | cavity nest |

Nesting material often consists of natural items found in the immediate area. Most nests consist of plant fibers (such as bark from grapevines), sticks, mud, dried grass, feathers, fur, or soft, fuzzy tufts from thistle. Some birds, including Black-chinned Hummingbirds, use spiderwebs to glue nest materials together.

Transportation of nesting material is limited to the amount a bird can hold or carry. Birds must make many trips afield to gather enough material to complete a nest. Most nests take four days or more, and hundreds, if not thousands, of trips to build.

A **ground nest** can be a mound of vegetation on the ground or in the water. It can also be just a simple, shallow depression scraped out in earth, stones or sand. Killdeer and Horned Larks scrape out ground nests without adding any nesting material.

The **platform nest** represents a much more complex type of construction. Typically built with twigs or sticks and branches, this nest forms a platform and has a depression in the center to nestle the eggs. Platform nests can be in trees; on balconies, cliffs, bridges, or man-made platforms; and even in flowerpots. They often provide space for the adventurous young and function as a landing platform for the parents.

Mourning Doves and herons don't anchor their platform nests to trees, so these can tumble from branches during high winds and storms. Hawks, eagles, ospreys and other birds construct sturdier platform nests with large sticks and branches.

Other platform nests are constructed on the ground with mud, grass and other vegetation from the area. Many waterfowl build platform nests on the ground near or in water. A **floating platform nest** moves with the water level, preventing the nest, eggs and birds from being flooded.

Three-quarters of all songbirds construct a **cup nest,** which is a modified platform nest. The supporting platform is built first and attached firmly to a tree, shrub, or rock ledge or the ground. Next, the sides are constructed with grass, small twigs, bark or leaves, which are woven together and often glued with mud for added strength. The inner cup can be lined with down feathers, animal fur or hair, or soft plant materials and is contoured last.

The **pendulous nest** is an unusual nest that looks like a sock hanging from a branch. Attached to the end of small branches of trees, this unique nest is inaccessible to most predators and often waves wildly in a breeze.

Woven tightly with plant fibers, the pendulous nest is strong and watertight and takes up to a week to build. A small opening at the top or on the side allows parents access to the grass-lined interior. More commonly used by tropical birds, this complex nest has also been mastered by orioles and kinglets. It must be one heck of a ride to be inside one of these nests during a windy spring thunderstorm!

The **cavity nest** is used by many species of birds, most notably woodpeckers and Western Bluebirds. A cavity nest is often excavated from a branch or tree trunk and offers shelter from storms, sun, cold and predators. A small entrance hole in a tree can lead to a nest chamber that is up to a safe 10 inches (25 cm) deep.

Typically made by woodpeckers, cavity nests are usually used only once by the builder. Nest cavities can be used for many subsequent years by such inhabitants as Wood Ducks, mergansers and bluebirds. Kingfishers, on the other hand, can dig a tunnel up to 4 feet (1 m) long in a riverbank. The nest chamber at the end of the tunnel is already well insulated, so it's usually only sparsely lined.

One of the most clever of all nests is the **no nest,** or daycare nest. Parasitic birds, such as Brown-headed Cowbirds, don't build their own nests. Instead, the egg-laden female searches out the nest of another bird and sneaks in to lay an egg while the host mother isn't looking.

A mother cowbird wastes no energy building a nest only to have it raided by a predator. Laying her eggs in the nests of other birds transfers the responsibility of raising her young to the host. When she lays her eggs in several nests, the chances increase that at least one of her babies will live to maturity.

Who Builds the Nest?

Generally, the female bird constructs the nest. She gathers the materials and does the building, with an occasional visit from her mate to check on progress. In some species, both parents contribute equally to nest building. The male may forage for sticks, grass or mud, but it is the female that often fashions the nest. Only rarely does a male build a nest by himself.

Fledging

Fledging is the time between hatching and flight, or leaving the nest. Some species of birds are **precocial,** meaning they leave the nest within hours of hatching, though it may be weeks before they can fly. This is common in waterfowl and shorebirds.

Baby birds that hatch naked and blind need to stay in the nest for a few weeks (these birds are **altricial**). Baby birds that are still in the nest are **nestlings.** Until birds start to fly, they are called **fledglings.**

Why Birds Migrate

Why do so many species of birds migrate? The short answer is simple: food. Birds migrate to locations with abundant food, as it is easier to breed where there is food than where food is scarce. Summer Tanagers, for instance, are **complete migrators** that fly from the tropics of South America to nest in the forests of North America, where billions of newly hatched insects are available to feed to their young.

Other migrators, such as some birds of prey, migrate back to northern regions in spring. In these locations, they hunt mice, voles and other small rodents that are beginning to breed.

Complete migrators have a set time and pattern of migration. Every year at nearly the same time, they head to a specific wintering ground. Complete migrators may travel great distances, sometimes 15,000 miles (24,100 km) or more in one year.

Complete migration doesn't necessarily imply flying from the cold, frozen northland to a tropical destination. The Black-chinned Hummingbird, for example, is a complete migrator that flies from Texas to spend the winter in Central and South America. This trip is still considered complete migration.

Complete migrators have many interesting aspects. In spring, males often leave a few weeks before the females, arriving early to scope out possibilities for nesting sites and food sources, and to begin to defend territories. The females arrive several weeks later. In many species, the females and their young leave earlier in the fall, often up to four weeks before the adult males.

Other species, such as the Lesser Goldfinch, are **partial migrators**. These birds usually wait until their food supplies dwindle before flying south. Unlike complete migrators, partial migrators move only far enough south, or sometimes east and west, to find abundant food. In some years it might be only a few hundred miles, while in other years it can be as much as a thousand. This kind of migration, dependent on weather and the availability of food, is sometimes called seasonal movement.

Unlike the predictable complete migrators or partial migrators, **irruptive migrators** can move every third to fifth year or, in some cases, in consecutive years. These migrations are triggered when times are tough and food is scarce. Red-breasted Nuthatches are irruptive migrators. They leave their normal northern range in search of more food or in response to overpopulation.

Many other birds don't migrate at all. Carolina Chickadees, for example, are **non-migrators** that remain in their habitat all year long and just move around as necessary to find food.

How Do Birds Migrate?

One of the many secrets of migration is fat. While most people are fighting the ongoing battle of the bulge, birds intentionally gorge themselves to gain as much fat as possible without losing the ability to fly. Fat provides the greatest amount of energy per unit of weight. In the same way that your car needs gas, birds are propelled by fat and stall without it.

During long migratory flights, fat deposits are used up quickly, and birds need to stop to refuel. This is when backyard bird feeding stations and undeveloped, natural spaces around our towns and cities are especially important. Some birds require up to 2–3 days of constant feeding to build their fat reserves before continuing their seasonal trip.

Many birds, such as most eagles, hawks, ospreys, falcons and vultures, migrate during the day. Larger birds can hold more body fat, go longer without eating and take longer to migrate. These birds glide along on rising columns of warm air, called thermals, that hold them aloft while they slowly make their way north or south. They generally rest at night and hunt early in the morning before the sun has a chance to warm the land and create good soaring conditions. Daytime migrators use a combination of landforms, rivers, and the rising and setting sun to guide them in the right direction.

The majority of small birds, called **passerines,** migrate at night. Studies show that some use the stars to navigate. Others use the setting sun, and still others, such as pigeons, use Earth's magnetic field to guide them north or south.

While flying at night may not seem like a good idea, it's actually safer. First, there are fewer avian predators hunting for birds at night. Second, night travel allows time during the day to find food in unfamiliar surroundings. Third, wind patterns at night tend to be flat, or laminar. Flat winds don't have the turbulence of daytime winds and can help push the smaller birds along.

HOW TO USE THIS GUIDE

To help you quickly and easily identify birds, this field guide is organized by color. Refer to the color key on the first page, note the color of the bird, and turn to that section. For example, the Red-headed Woodpecker is black and white with a red head. Because the bird is mostly black-and-white, it will be found in the black-and-white section.

Each color section is also arranged by size, generally with the smaller birds first. Sections may also incorporate the average size in a range, which in some cases reflects size differences between male and female birds. Flip through the pages in the color section to find the bird. If you already know the name of the bird, check the index for the page number.

In some species, the male and female are very different in color. In others, the breeding and winter plumage colors differ. These species will have an inset photograph with a page reference and will be found in two color sections.

You will find a variety of information in the bird description sections. To learn more, turn to the sample on pp. 22–23.

Range Maps

Range maps are included for each bird. Colored areas indicate where the bird is frequently found. The colors represent the presence of a species during a specific season, not the density, or amount, of birds in the area. Green is used for summer, blue for winter, red for year-round and yellow for migration.

While every effort has been made to depict accurate ranges, these are constantly in flux due to a variety of factors. Changing weather, habitat, species abundance and availability of vital resources, such as food and water, can affect the migration and movement of local populations, causing birds to be found in areas that are atypical for the species. So please use the maps as intended—as general guides only.

female
p. 147

male

Common Name

YEAR-ROUND
SUMMER
MIGRATION
WINTER

Size: measurement is from head to tip of tail; wingspan may be listed as well

Male: brief description of the male bird; may include breeding, winter or other plumages

Female: brief description of the female bird, which is sometimes different from the male

Juvenile: brief description of the juvenile bird, which often looks like the adult female

Nest: kind of nest the bird builds to raise its young; who builds it; number of broods per year

Eggs: number of eggs you might expect to see in a nest; color and marking

Incubation: average days the parents spend incubating the eggs; who does the incubation

Fledging: average days the young spend in the nest after hatching but before they leave the nest; who does the most "childcare" and feeding

Migration: type of migrator: complete (seasonal, consistent), partial (seasonal, destination varies), irruptive (unpredictable, depends on the food supply) or non-migrator

Food: what the bird eats most of the time (e.g., seeds, insects, fruit, nectar, small mammals, fish) and whether it typically comes to a bird feeder

Compare: notes about other birds that look similar and the pages on which they can be found; may include extra information to aid in identification

Stan's Notes: Interesting natural history information. This could be something to look or listen for or something to help positively identify the bird. Also includes remarkable features.

23

female
p. 165

male

Bronzed
Cowbird

YEAR-ROUND

Brown-headed Cowbird
Molothrus ater

Size: 7½" (19 cm)

Male: Glossy black with a chocolate-brown head. Dark eyes. Pointed, sharp gray bill.

Female: dull brown with a pointed, sharp, gray bill

Juvenile: similar to female but with dull-gray plumage and a streaked chest

Nest: no nest; lays eggs in nests of other birds

Eggs: 5–7; white with brown markings

Incubation: 10–13 days; host bird incubates eggs

Fledging: 10–11 days; host birds feed the young

Migration: non-migrator in Texas

Food: insects, seeds; will come to seed feeders

Compare: The male Red-winged Blackbird (p. 31) is slightly larger with red-and-yellow patches on upper wings. Common Grackle (p. 35) has a long tail and lacks the brown head. European Starling (p. 27) has a shorter tail.

Stan's Notes: Cowbirds are members of the blackbird family. One of two species of parasitic birds in Texas. The other, the Bronzed Cowbird (see inset), is easily identified by its bright-red eyes. Brood parasites lay their eggs in the nests of other birds, leaving the host birds to raise their young. Cowbirds are known to have laid their eggs in the nests of over 200 species of birds. While some birds reject cowbird eggs, most incubate them and raise the young, even to the exclusion of their own. Look for warblers and other birds feeding young birds twice their own size. Named "Cowbird" for its habit of following bison and cattle herds to feed on insects flushed up by the animals.

winter

breeding

European Starling
Sturnus vulgaris

YEAR-ROUND

Size: 7½" (19 cm)

Male: Glittering, iridescent purplish black in spring and summer; duller and speckled with white in fall and winter. Long, pointed, yellow bill in spring; gray in fall. Pointed wings. Short tail.

Female: same as male

Juvenile: similar to adults, with grayish-brown plumage and a streaked chest

Nest: cavity; male and female line cavity; 2 broods per year

Eggs: 4–6; bluish with brown markings

Incubation: 12–14 days; female and male incubate

Fledging: 18–20 days; female and male feed the young

Migration: non-migrator

Food: insects, seeds, fruit; visits seed or suet feeders

Compare: The Common Grackle (p. 35) has a long tail. The male Brown-headed Cowbird (p. 25) has a brown head. Look for the shiny, dark feathers to help identify the European Starling.

Stan's Notes: One of our most numerous songbirds. Mimics the songs of up to 20 bird species and imitates sounds, including the human voice. Jaws are more powerful when opening than when closing, enabling the bird to pry open crevices to find insects. Often displaces woodpeckers, chickadees and other cavity-nesting birds. Large families gather with blackbirds in the fall. Not a native bird; 100 starlings were introduced to New York City in 1890–91 from Europe. Bill changes color in spring and fall.

female
p. 183

Eastern
Towhee

Spotted Towhee

Pipilo maculatus

YEAR-ROUND
WINTER

Size: 8½" (22 cm)

Male: Mostly black with dirty red-brown sides and a white belly. Multiple white spots on wings and sides. Long black tail with a white tip. Rich, red eyes.

Female: very similar to male but with a brown head

Juvenile: brown with a heavily streaked chest

Nest: cup; female builds; 1–2 broods per year

Eggs: 3–5; white with brown markings

Incubation: 12–14 days; female and male incubate

Fledging: 10–12 days; female and male feed young

Migration: partial migrator to non-migrator

Food: seeds, fruit, insects

Compare: Closely related to the Green-tailed Towhee (p. 357), which lacks the bold black and red colors. Smaller than American Robin (p. 315).

Stan's Notes: The Spotted Towhee and Eastern Towhee were once considered a single species called Rufous-sided Towhee. Found in a variety of habitats, from thick brush and chaparral to suburban backyards. Usually heard noisily scratching through dead leaves on the ground for food. Over 70 percent of its diet is plant material. Eats more insects during spring and summer. Well known to retreat from danger by walking away rather than taking to flight. Nest is nearly always on the ground under bushes but away from where the male perches to sing. Begins breeding in April. Lays eggs in May. After the breeding season, moves to higher elevations. Song and plumage vary geographically and aren't well studied or understood.

female
p. 181

male

Red-winged Blackbird
Agelaius phoeniceus

YEAR-ROUND

Size:	8½" (22 cm)
Male:	Jet black with red-and-yellow patches (epaulets) on upper wings. Pointed black bill.
Female:	heavily streaked brown with a pointed brown bill and white eyebrows
Juvenile:	same as female
Nest:	cup; female builds; 2–3 broods per year
Eggs:	3–4; bluish green with brown markings
Incubation:	10–12 days; female incubates
Fledging:	11–14 days; female and male feed the young
Migration:	non-migrator to partial migrator
Food:	seeds, insects; visits seed and suet feeders
Compare:	The male Brown-headed Cowbird (p. 25) is smaller and glossier and has a brown head. The bold red-and-yellow epaulets distinguish the male Red-winged from other blackbirds.

Stan's Notes: One of the most widespread and numerous birds in Texas. Found around marshes, wetlands, lakes and rivers. Flocks with as many as 10,000 birds have been reported. Males arrive before the females and sing to defend their territory. The male repeats his call from the top of a cattail while showing off his red-and-yellow shoulder patches. The female chooses a mate and often builds her nest over shallow water in a thick stand of cattails. The male can be aggressive when defending the nest. Red-winged Blackbirds feed mostly on seeds in spring and fall, and insects throughout the summer.

female
p. 191

male

MIGRATION
WINTER

Yellow-headed Blackbird
Xanthocephalus xanthocephalus

Size: 9–11" (23–28 cm)

Male: Large black bird with a lemon-yellow head, breast and nape of neck. Black mask and gray bill. White wing patches.

Female: similar to male but slightly smaller with a brown body and dull-yellow head and chest

Juvenile: similar to female

Nest: cup; female builds; 2 broods per year

Eggs: 3–5; greenish white with brown markings

Incubation: 11–13 days; female incubates

Fledging: 9–12 days; female feeds the young

Migration: complete, to western parts of Texas, Mexico

Food: insects, seeds; will come to ground feeders

Compare: The male Red-winged Blackbird (p. 31) is smaller and has red-and-yellow patches on its wings. Look for the bright-yellow head to identify the male Yellow-headed.

Stan's Notes: Found around marshes, wetland and lakes. Nests in deep water, unlike its cousin, the Red-winged Blackbird, which prefers shallow water. Usually heard before seen. Gives a raspy, low, metallic-sounding call. The male is the only large black bird with a bright-yellow head. He gives an impressive mating display, flying with his head drooped and feet and tail pointing down while steadily beating his wings. Young keep low and out of sight for up to three weeks before they start to fly. Migrates in large flocks of as many as 200 birds, often with Red-winged Blackbirds and Brown-headed Cowbirds. Flocks of mainly males return in early April; females return later. Most colonies consist of 20–100 nests.

Common Grackle
Quiscalus quiscula

YEAR-ROUND

Size: 11–13" (28–33 cm)

Male: Large, iridescent blackbird with bluish-black head and purplish-brown body. Long black tail. Long, thin bill and bright-golden eyes.

Female: similar to male but smaller and duller

Juvenile: similar to female

Nest: cup; female builds; 2 broods per year

Eggs: 4–5; greenish white with brown markings

Incubation: 13–14 days; female incubates

Fledging: 16–20 days; female and male feed the young

Migration: non-migrator to partial in Texas; will move around to find food

Food: fruit, seeds, insects; will come to seed and suet feeders

Compare: Male Boat-tailed Grackle (p. 41) is larger and has a much longer tail. The European Starling (p. 27) is much smaller with a speckled appearance, and a yellow bill during breeding season. Male Red-winged Blackbird (p. 31) has red-and-yellow wing markings (epaulets).

Stan's Notes: Usually nests in small colonies of up to 75 pairs but travels with other blackbird species in large flocks. Known to feed in farm fields. The common name is derived from the Latin word *gracula*, meaning "jackdaw," another species of bird and a term that can refer to any bird in the *Quiscalus* genus. The male holds his tail in a deep V shape during flight. The flight pattern is usually level, as opposed to an undulating movement. Unlike most birds, it has larger muscles for opening its mouth than for closing it, enabling it to pry crevices apart to find hidden insects.

Common Gallinule
Gallinula galeata

YEAR-ROUND
SUMMER

Size: 13–15" (33–38 cm)

Male: Nearly black overall with yellow-tipped red bill. Red forehead. Thin line of white along sides. Yellowish-green legs.

Female: same as male

Juvenile: same as adult, but brown with white throat and dirty-yellow legs

Nest: ground; female and male build; 1–2 broods per year

Eggs: 2–10; brown with dark markings

Incubation: 19–22 days; female and male incubate

Fledging: 40–50 days; female and male feed the young

Migration: partial migrator to non-migrator in Texas

Food: insects, snails, seeds, green leaves, fruit

Compare: American Coot (p. 39) is similar in size but lacks the distinctive yellow-tipped bill and red forehead of Common Gallinule. Purple Gallinule (p. 125) is similar in size but has an iridescent blue-and-green body.

Stan's Notes: Also known as Mud Hen or Pond Chicken. A nearly all-black duck-like bird often seen in freshwater marshes and lakes. Walks on floating vegetation or swims while hunting for insects. Females known to lay eggs in other gallinule nests in addition to their own. Builds its nest with cattails and bulrushes and sometimes takes an old nest in a low shrub. A cooperative breeder, having young of first brood help raise young of second. Young leave nest usually within a few hours after hatching, but stay with the family for a couple months. Young ride on backs of adults.

American Coot
Fulica americana

YEAR-ROUND

Size: 13–16" (33–40 cm)

Male: Gray-to-black waterbird. Duck-like white bill with a dark band near the tip and a small red patch near the eyes. Small white patch near base of tail. Green legs and feet. Red eyes.

Female: same as male

Juvenile: much paler than adults, with a gray bill

Nest: floating platform; female and male construct; 1 brood per year

Eggs: 9–12; pinkish buff with brown markings

Incubation: 21–25 days; female and male incubate

Fledging: 49–52 days; female and male feed young

Migration: non-migrator in Texas

Food: insects, aquatic plants

Compare: Smaller than most waterfowl, it is the only black, duck-like bird with a white bill.

Stan's Notes: Usually seen in large flocks on open water. Not a duck, as it has large lobed toes instead of webbed feet. An excellent diver and swimmer, bobbing its head as it swims. A favorite food of Bald Eagles. It is not often seen in flight, unless it's trying to escape from an eagle. To take off, it scrambles across the surface of the water, flapping its wings. Gives a unique series of creaks, groans and clicks. Anchors its floating platform nest to vegetation. Huge flocks with as many as 1,000 birds gather for migration. Migrates at night. The common name "Coot" comes from the Middle English word *coote*, which was used to describe various waterfowl. Also called Mud Hen.

female
p. 207

male

Boat-tailed Grackle
Quiscalus major

YEAR-ROUND

Size: 15–17" (38–43 cm), male
13–15" (33–38 cm), female

Male: Iridescent blue-black bird. Dark eyes. Very long keel-shaped tail.

Female: brown version of male, lacks iridescence

Juvenile: similar to female

Nest: cup; female builds; 2 broods per year

Eggs: 2–4; pale greenish blue with brown marks

Incubation: 13–15 days; female incubates

Fledging: 12–15 days; female feeds the young

Migration: non-migrator; moves around to find food

Food: insects, berries, seeds, fish; visits feeders

Compare: Male Common Grackle (p. 35) lacks Boat-tailed's distinctive long tail. Similar size as male Great-tailed Grackle (p. 43), which is more common and widespread. Look for an iridescent blue head and a very long tail to identify the Boat-tailed.

Stan's Notes: A noisy bird of coastal saltwater and inland marshes, giving several harsh, high-pitched calls and several squeaks. Eats a wide variety of foods, from grains to fish. Sometimes seen picking insects off the backs of cattle. Will also visit bird feeders. Makes a cup nest with mud or cow dung and grass. Nests in small colonies. Most nesting occurs in April and May. Boat-taileds in Texas and on the Gulf Coast have dark eyes. Birds further east, on the Atlantic Coast, have bright-red eyes.

female
p. 209

male

Great-tailed Grackle

Quiscalus mexicanus

YEAR-ROUND

Size: 18" (45 cm), male
15" (38 cm), female

Male: Large all-black bird with iridescent purple sheen on the head and back. Exceptionally long tail. Bright-yellow eyes.

Female: considerably smaller than the male, overall brown bird with gray-to-brown belly, light-brown-to-white eyes, eyebrows, throat and upper chest

Juvenile: similar to female

Nest: cup; female builds; 1–2 broods per year

Eggs: 3–5; greenish blue with brown markings

Incubation: 12–14 days; female incubates

Fledging: 21–23 days; female feeds young

Migration: non-migrator to partial in Texas; will move around to find food

Food: insects, fruit, seeds; comes to seed feeders

Compare: Common Grackle (p. 35) is smaller, with a much shorter tail. Male Brown-headed Cowbird (p. 25) lacks the long tail and has a brown head. The male Boat-tailed Grackle (p. 41) is found along the coast.

Stan's Notes: This is our largest grackle. It was once considered a subspecies of the Boat-tailed Grackle. A colony nester. Males do not participate in nest building, incubation or raising young. Males rarely fight; females squabble over nest sites and materials. Several females mate with one male. The species is expanding northward, moving into northern states. Western populations tend to be larger than eastern. Song varies from population to population.

in flight

American Crow
Corvus brachyrhynchos

YEAR-ROUND

Size: 18" (45 cm)

Male: All-black bird with black bill, legs and feet. Can have a purple sheen in direct sunlight.

Female: same as male

Juvenile: same as adult

Nest: platform; female builds; 1 brood per year

Eggs: 4–6; bluish to olive-green with brown marks

Incubation: 18 days; female incubates

Fledging: 28–35 days; female and male feed the young

Migration: non-migrator to partial migrator

Food: fruit, insects, mammals, fish, carrion; will come to seed and suet feeders

Compare: Chihuahuan Raven (p. 47) and Common Raven (p. 49) are similar, but they have a larger bill and have shaggy throat feathers. Crow's call is higher than the raspy, low calls of ravens. Crow has a squared tail. Ravens have wedge-shaped tails, apparent in flight.

Stan's Notes: One of the most recognizable birds in Texas, found in most habitats. Imitates other birds and human voices. One of the smartest of all birds and very social, often entertaining itself by provoking chases with other birds. Eats roadkill but is rarely hit by vehicles. Can live as long as 20 years. Often reuses its nest every year if it's not taken over by a Great Horned Owl. Unmated birds, known as helpers, help to raise the young. Extended families roost together at night, dispersing daily to hunt. Cannot soar on thermals; flaps constantly and glides downward. Gathers in huge communal flocks of up to 10,000 birds in winter.

Chihuahuan Raven

Corvus cryptoleucus

YEAR-ROUND

Size: 20" (50 cm)

Male: Large all-black bird with a large black bill. Long bristle-like feathers cover more than half the length of the bill. Slightly shaggy throat feathers. Black legs and feet.

Female: same as male

Juvenile: similar to adult, but color of feathers on the neck is sometimes lighter

Nest: cup; female builds; 1 brood per year

Eggs: 5–7; gray to green with brown markings

Incubation: 19–21 days; female and male incubate

Fledging: 28–30 days; female and male feed young

Migration: partial migrator to non-migrator, to Mexico

Food: seeds, leaves, insects, fruit, small mammals

Compare: Common Raven (p. 49) is very similar but it is larger and has a larger and longer bill. The American Crow (p. 45) lacks the shaggy throat and has a smaller bill.

Stan's Notes: Often confused with crows and other ravens. Usually found in open, flat regions. Known to cache food. Male performs an impressive aerial display, soaring and tumbling, then standing in front of female with neck feathers fluffed. Builds a loose cup nest of sticks and lines it with hair and dry grass. Nest is usually solitary in a tree. Will reuse its nest several years in a row. Often breeds late in the season, presumably to time hatching with the flush of insects after the rainy season. Forms large flocks of up to several hundred after young leave the nest and throughout the winter.

in flight

Common Raven
Corvus corax

YEAR-ROUND

Size: 22–27" (56–69 cm)

Male: Large all-black bird with a shaggy beard of feathers on throat and chin. Large black bill. Large wedge-shaped tail, best seen in flight.

Female: same as male

Juvenile: same as adult

Nest: platform; female and male construct; 1 brood per year

Eggs: 4–6; pale green with brown markings

Incubation: 18–21 days; female incubates

Fledging: 38–44 days; female and male feed the young

Migration: non-migrator in Texas, will move around to find food

Food: insects, fruit, small animals, carrion

Compare: Chihuahuan Raven (p. 47) is similar but smaller. American Crow (p. 45) is smaller and lacks the shaggy throat feathers. Low raspy call, compared with the higher-pitched call of the Chihuahuan Raven and Crow.

Stan's Notes: Considered by some people to be the smartest of all birds. Known for its aerial acrobatics and long swooping dives. Soars on wind without flapping, like a raptor. Sometimes scavenges with crows and gulls. A cooperative hunter that often communicates the location of a good source of food to other ravens. Most start to breed at 3–4 years. Complex courtship includes grabbing bills, preening each other and cooing. Long-term pair bond. Uses the same nest site for many years.

drying

juvenile

soaring

Black Vulture
Coragyps atratus

YEAR-ROUND

Size: 25–28" (63–71 cm); up to 5¼' wingspan

Male: Black with dark-gray head and legs. Short tail. In flight, all black with light-gray wing tips.

Female: same as male

Juvenile: similar to adult

Nest: no nest, on a stump or on ground, or takes an abandoned nest; 1 brood per year

Eggs: 1–3; light green with dark markings

Incubation: 37–45 days; female and male incubate

Fledging: 75–80 days; female and male feed the young

Migration: non-migrator

Food: carrion; occasionally will capture small live mammals

Compare: Turkey Vulture (p. 53) is slightly larger, with a bright-red head. Turkey Vulture has two-toned wings with a black leading edge and light-gray trailing edge. The Black Vulture has shorter, gray-tipped wings and a shorter tail.

Stan's Notes: Also called Black Buzzard. A more gregarious bird than the Turkey Vulture. In flight, the Black Vulture holds its wings straight out to its sides unlike the Turkey Vulture, which holds its wings in a V pattern. More aggressive while feeding but less skilled at finding carrion than the Turkey Vulture, it is thought the Black Vulture's sense of smell is less developed. Families stay together up to a year. Often nests and roosts with other Black Vultures. If startled, especially at the nest, it regurgitates with power and accuracy. Like other vultures, it often spreads its wings to warm up in the morning or dry out after a rain.

soaring

juvenile

drying

Turkey Vulture
Cathartes aura

YEAR-ROUND
SUMMER

Size: 26–32" (66–80 cm); up to 6' wingspan

Male: Large and black with a naked red head and legs. In flight, wings are two-toned with a black leading edge and a gray trailing edge. Wing tips end in finger-like projections. Tail is long and squared. Ivory bill.

Female: same as male but slightly smaller

Juvenile: similar to adults, with a gray-to-blackish head and bill

Nest: no nest or minimal nest, on a cliff or in a cave, sometimes in a hollow tree; 1 brood per year

Eggs: 1–3; white with brown markings

Incubation: 38–41 days; female and male incubate

Fledging: 66–88 days; female and male feed the young

Migration: non-migrator to partial migrator in Texas

Food: carrion; parents regurgitate to feed the young

Compare: Black Vulture (p. 51) has shorter wings and tail. Bald Eagle (p. 103) is larger and lacks two-toned wings. Look for the obvious naked red head to identify the Turkey Vulture.

Stan's Notes: The naked head reduces the risk of feather fouling (picking up diseases) from contact with carcasses. It has a strong bill for tearing apart flesh. Unlike hawks and eagles, it has weak feet more suited for walking than grasping. One of the few birds with a developed sense of smell. Mostly mute, making only grunts and groans. Holds its wings in an upright V shape in flight. Teeters from wing tip to wing tip as it soars and hovers. Seen in trees with wings outstretched, sunning itself and drying after a rain.

in flight

juvenile

Neotropic
Cormorant

crests

drying

Double-crested Cormorant

Phalacrocorax auritus

YEAR-ROUND
WINTER

Size: 31–35" (79–89 cm); up to 4⅓' wingspan

Male: Large black waterbird with unusual blue-teal eyes and a long, snake-like neck. Large gray bill, with yellow at the base and a hooked tip.

Female: same as male

Juvenile: lighter brown with a grayish chest and neck

Nest: platform; male and female construct; 1 brood per year

Eggs: 3–4; bluish white without markings

Incubation: 25–29 days; female and male incubate

Fledging: 37–42 days; male and female feed the young

Migration: complete, to Texas, Mexico, Central America

Food: small fish, aquatic insects

Compare: Male Anhinga (p. 57) has white spots and streaks and a long straight bill without a hooked tip. The Turkey Vulture (p. 53) is similar in size and also perches on branches with wings open to dry in sun, but it has a naked red head.

Stan's Notes: Flocks fly in a large V or a line. Swims underwater to catch fish, holding its wings at its sides. This bird's outer feathers soak up water, but its body feathers don't. To dry off, it strikes an upright pose with wings outstretched, facing the sun. Gives grunts, pops and groans. Named "Double-crested" for the crests on its head, which are not often seen. "Cormorant" is a contraction from *corvus marinus*, meaning "crow" or "raven," and "of the sea." The Neotropic Cormorant (see inset) is found along the Gulf Coast. It is smaller and thinner than Double-crested, and adult Neotropic has a white mark at base of bill. Map shows combined range.

male

female

juvenile

Anhinga
Anhinga anhinga

Size: 33–37" (84–94 cm); up to 3¾' wingspan

Male: All black with glossy green-and-white spots and streaks on shoulders and wings. Long neck and tail. Long, narrow yellow bill.

Female: similar to male, buff-brown neck and breast

Juvenile: similar to female, light-brown-to-white body

Nest: platform; female and male build; 1 brood per year

Eggs: 2–4; light blue without markings

Incubation: 26–29 days; female and male incubate

Fledging: 21–25 days; female and male feed the young

Migration: complete to non-migrator, to coastal Texas and Mexico

Food: fish, aquatic insects, crustaceans and small mammals

Compare: The Double-crested Cormorant (p. 55) is slightly smaller and lacks the white spots and streaks of male Anhinga. Cormorant has a shorter bill with a curved tip unlike the long straight bill of the Anhinga.

YEAR-ROUND
SUMMER

Stan's Notes: Also called Snakebird due to its habit of appearing like a snake—surfacing with just its head and long thin neck showing above the water. It skewers fish, a favorite prey, with its long sharp bill. Unlike ducks and other diving birds, its feathers become waterlogged, which helps it when diving and maneuvering underwater. Afterward, it often strikes a pose with wings spread to dry in the sun (see photo). A strong flier and frequently seen soaring, it is confused with birds of prey. In flight, the long neck and tail help to identify it.

female
p. 157

breeding male

non-breeding
male

Lark Bunting
Calamospiza melanocorys

Size: 6½" (16 cm)

Male: Short, stocky black bird with a large broad head. White wing patches and large bluish-gray bill. Winter male is black, brown, gray and white-striped with white wing patches.

Female: overall brown with a heavily streaked chest, white belly, black vertical line on each side of white chin, may have a dark central spot on the chest, faint white eyebrows

Juvenile: similar to adult of the same sex

Nest: cup; female builds; 1–2 broods per year

Eggs: 4–6; pale blue with markings

Incubation: 11–13 days; female and male incubate

Fledging: 8–12 days; female and male feed young

Migration: complete, to most of Texas, Mexico

Food: insects, seeds

Compare: The breeding male's bold black-and-white plumage is hard to confuse with any other bird's. Look for the rather large broad head and large bill to help identify.

SUMMER
WINTER

Stan's Notes: Common in the dry plains and sagebrush regions of the state. Has short rounded wings. Flying with shallow wingbeats, the male flashes white wing patches. Male takes to air to display to female, setting its wings in a V position and floating back, rocking like a butterfly, singing a most amazing song. Song is like the song of Old World larks, hence the common name. Will flock in fall with hundreds, if not thousands, of other Lark Buntings for migration.

male

female

YEAR-ROUND

Downy Woodpecker
Dryobates pubescens

Size: 6½" (15 cm)

Male: Small woodpecker with a white belly and black-and-white spotted wings. Red mark on the back of the head and a white stripe down the back. Short black bill.

Female: same as male but lacks the red mark

Juvenile: same as female, some with a red mark near the forehead

Nest: cavity with a round entrance hole; male and female excavate; 1 brood per year

Eggs: 3–5; white without markings

Incubation: 11–12 days; female incubates during the day, male incubates at night

Fledging: 20–25 days; male and female feed the young

Migration: non-migrator

Food: insects, seeds; visits seed and suet feeders

Compare: The Hairy Woodpecker (p. 69) is larger. Look for the Downy's shorter, thinner bill.

Stan's Notes: Abundant and widespread where trees are present. This is perhaps the most common woodpecker in the U.S. Stiff tail feathers help to brace it like a tripod as it clings to a tree. Like other woodpeckers, it has a long, barbed tongue to pull insects from tiny places. Mates drum on branches or hollow logs to announce territory, which is rarely larger than 5 acres (2 ha). Repeats a high-pitched "peek-peek" call. Nest cavity is wider at the bottom than at the top and is lined with fallen wood chips. Male performs most of the brooding. During winter, it will roost in a cavity. Doesn't breed in high elevations but often moves there in winter for food. Undulates in flight.

male

female

Ladder-backed Woodpecker

Dryobates scalaris

YEAR-ROUND

Size:	7" (18 cm)
Male:	Horizontal black-and-white zebra stripes on back, wings and tail. Tan breast and belly with black spots. Red crown. Black eye stripe and mustache mark. Dark bill.
Female:	same as male, but lacks a red crown
Juvenile:	similar to female
Nest:	cavity; female and male excavate, then use wood chips to line hole; 1 brood per year
Eggs:	2–4; white without markings
Incubation:	13–15 days; female and male incubate
Fledging:	14–16 days; female and male feed young
Migration:	non-migrator
Food:	insects, fruit
Compare:	Male Red-bellied Woodpecker (p. 73) has a red crown and zebra stripes on its back, but its red crown extends down the nape. Golden-fronted Woodpecker (p. 75) has a tan chest, black wing tips and a yellow patch at the base of the upper bill.

Stan's Notes: Less common than other woodpeckers of arid desert scrub. Often probes for insects and larvae or feeds on cactus fruit. Male often feeds closer to ground than female; jumping to the ground to grab an insect or pecks at the base of shrubs and trees. Female feeds higher up and probes less, pulling bugs from leaves or cracks in bark. A sharp "peek" call and short spurt of drumming. Will drum on a log or tree to advertise territory ownership. Nests in dead branches of mesquite or saguaro cactus. Common name comes from the ladder-like black-and-white stripes.

Black Phoebe
Sayornis nigricans

YEAR-ROUND

Size: 7" (18 cm)

Male: Black head, neck, breast and back with a white belly and undertail. Long narrow tail. Dark eyes, bill and legs. Can raise and lower its small crest.

Female: same as male

Juvenile: similar to adult, brown-to-tan wing bars

Nest: cup; female builds; 1–2 broods per year

Eggs: 3–6; white without markings

Incubation: 15–17 days; female incubates

Fledging: 14–21 days; female and male feed young

Migration: partial migrator to non-migrator; will move around after breeding to find food

Food: insects

Compare: Distinctive black-and-white pattern makes identification easy. Watch for tail to pump up and down very quickly when perched. Similar in size to Eastern Phoebe (p. 297), which is gray.

Stan's Notes: Often seen in shrubby areas near water. Feeds mostly on insects near the surface of water. In the winter it feeds on insects near the ground. Like other flycatchers, perches on thin branches, flies out to snatch a passing insect and returns to perch. Pumps or bobs tail up and down quickly while perching. Male performs an aerial song and flight with a slow descent to attract a mate. Female builds shallow nest of mud, adhered to rocks or bridges, lined with hair and grass. Often uses same nest or location for several years.

male

female

WINTER

Yellow-bellied Sapsucker
Sphyrapicus varius

Size: 8–9" (20–23 cm)

Male: Checkered back with a red forehead, crown and chin. Yellow to tan on the chest and belly. White wing patches are seen flashing in flight.

Female: similar to male but with a white chin

Juvenile: similar to female, dull brown and lacks any red marking

Nest: cavity; female and male excavate, often in a live tree; 1 brood per year

Eggs: 5–6; white without markings

Incubation: 12–13 days; female incubates during the day, male incubates at night

Fledging: 25–29 days; female and male feed the young

Migration: complete migrator, to most parts of Texas, Mexico and Central America

Food: insects, tree sap; comes to suet feeders

Compare: The Red-headed Woodpecker (p. 71) has an all-red head. Look for the red chin and crown to identify the male Sapsucker, and the white chin and red crown to identify the female.

Stan's Notes: Found in small woods, forests, and suburban and rural areas. Drills rows of holes in trees to bleed the sap. Oozing sap attracts bugs, which it also eats. Defends its sapping sites from other birds that try to drink from the taps. Does not suck sap; rather, it laps the sticky liquid with its long, bristly tongue. A quiet bird, it makes few vocalizations but will meow like a cat. Drums on hollow branches, but unlike other woodpeckers, its rhythm is irregular. Makes short undulating flights with rapid wingbeats.

male

female

Hairy Woodpecker
Leuconotopicus villosus

YEAR-ROUND

Size: 9" (23 cm)

Male: Black-and-white woodpecker with a white belly. Black wings with rows of white spots. White stripe down the back. Long black bill. Red mark on the back of the head.

Female: same as male but lacks the red mark

Juvenile: grayer version of the female

Nest: cavity with an oval entrance hole; female and male excavate; 1 brood per year

Eggs: 3–6; white without markings

Incubation: 11–15 days; female incubates during the day, male incubates at night

Fledging: 28–30 days; male and female feed the young

Migration: non-migrator

Food: insects, nuts, seeds; comes to seed and suet feeders

Compare: Downy Woodpecker (p. 61) is much smaller and has a much shorter bill. Look for Hairy Woodpecker's long bill. Ladder-backed (p. 63) has black-and-white zebra stripes on the back.

Stan's Notes: A common bird in wooded backyards. Announces its arrival with a sharp chirp before landing on feeders. Responsible for eating many destructive forest insects. Uses its barbed tongue to extract insects from trees. Tiny, bristle-like feathers at the base of the bill protect the nostrils from wood dust. Drums on hollow logs, branches or stovepipes in spring to announce territory. Prefers to excavate nest cavities in live trees. Excavates a larger, more-oval-shaped entrance than the round entrance hole of the Downy Woodpecker. Makes short flights from tree to tree.

juvenile

YEAR-ROUND

Red-headed Woodpecker
Melanerpes erythrocephalus

Size: 9" (22.5 cm)

Male: All-red head with a solid black back. White chest, belly and rump. Black wings with large white wing patches seen flashing in flight. Black tail. Gray legs and bill.

Female: same as male

Juvenile: gray brown with white chest, lacks any red

Nest: cavity; male builds with help from female; 1 brood per year

Eggs: 4–5; white without markings

Incubation: 12–13 days; female and male incubate

Fledging: 27–30 days; female and male feed the young

Migration: partial migrator to non-migrator; will move to areas with an abundant supply of nuts

Food: insects, nuts, fruit; visits suet and seed feeders

Compare: No other woodpecker in Texas has an all-red head. The Pileated Woodpecker (p. 95) is the only other woodpecker with a solid black back, but it has a partial red head.

Stan's Notes: One of the few non-dimorphic woodpeckers, with males and females that look alike. Bill is strong enough to excavate a nest cavity only in soft, dead trees. Prefers open woodlands or woodland edges with many dead or rotting branches. Nests later than its close relative, the Red-bellied Woodpecker (p. 73), and will often take its cavity, if vacant. Unlike other woodpeckers, which use nest cavities just once briefly, it may use the same cavity for several years in a row. Often perches on top of dead snags. Stores acorns and other nuts. Gives a shrill, hoarse "churr" call.

male

female

Red-bellied Woodpecker

Melanerpes carolinus

YEAR-ROUND

Size: 9–9½" (23–24 cm)

Male: Black-and-white "zebra-backed" woodpecker with a white rump. Red crown extends down the nape of the neck. Tan chest. Pale-red tinge on the belly, often hard to see.

Female: same as male but with a light-gray crown and a red nape

Juvenile: gray version of adults; lacks a red crown and red nape

Nest: cavity; female and male excavate; 1 brood per year

Eggs: 4–5; white without markings

Incubation: 12–14 days; female incubates during the day, male incubates at night

Fledging: 24–27 days; female and male feed the young

Migration: non-migrator; moves around to find food

Food: insects, nuts, fruit; visits suet and seed feeders

Compare: Northern Flicker (p. 197) has a black bib on its belly, not a reddish wash. Male Golden-fronted Woodpecker (p. 75) has a red crown and zebra striping on its back, but also has a yellow patch at the base of the upper bill.

Stan's Notes: Likes shady woodlands, forest edges and backyards. Digs holes in rotten wood to find spiders, centipedes, and beetles. Hammers acorns and berries into crevices of trees for winter food. Returns to the same tree to excavate a new nest below that of the previous year. Undulating flight with rapid wingbeats. Gives a loud "querrr" call and a low "chug-chug-chug." Named for the pale red tinge on its belly. Expanding its range all over the country.

male

female

Golden-fronted Woodpecker
Melanerpes aurifrons

YEAR-ROUND

Size: 9½" (24 cm)

Male: Black and white zebra-patterned back with white rump. Black wing tips and tip of tail. Gray head, red crown and yellow-to-orange nape. Yellow patch at base of upper bill.

Female: same as male, but lacks the red crown

Juvenile: similar to female, but has a streaked breast and smaller yellow patch near upper bill

Nest: cavity; female and male excavate; 1–2 broods per year

Eggs: 4–7; white to cream without markings

Incubation: 12–14 days; female and male incubate, the female during day, male at night

Fledging: 28–30 days; female and male feed young

Migration: non-migrator; moves around to find food

Food: insects, nuts, seeds, berries; comes to seed and suet feeders

Compare: Male Red-bellied Woodpecker (p. 73) is similar, but has a red nape. Red-headed Woodpecker (p. 71) lacks the black-and-white back and has an entirely red head. Male Ladder-backed Woodpecker (p. 63) has zebra striping on back, black spots on belly and a black eye stripe and mustache.

Stan's Notes: Named for the yellow patch near bill. Often alone or in pairs. Prefers dry forests, cottonwoods near water and mesquite habitat. Will use a nest box stuffed with sawdust. Less vocal than other woodpeckers. Caches food in crevices in bark. Hybridizes with Red-bellied Woodpeckers where ranges overlap.

male

female

Scissor-tailed Flycatcher
Tyrannus forficatus

SUMMER

Size: 10" (24 cm)

Male: White-to-gray head, neck, breast and back. Black wings with bright pink wing linings, seen in flight. Faint pink coloring on flanks and belly. An extremely long black tail with patches of white.

Female: similar to male, with a much shorter tail

Juvenile: similar to adults, with a shorter tail, lacking pink underwings and sides

Nest: cup; female builds; 1 brood per year

Eggs: 3–5; white with brown and red markings

Incubation: 14–17 days; female incubates

Fledging: 14–16 days; female and male feed young

Migration: complete, to Central and South America

Food: insects

Compare: This flycatcher's extremely long tail and the distinctive black-and-white pattern with its pink wing linings make it hard to confuse with any other bird.

Stan's Notes: A wonderful summer resident. Like most flycatchers, it hunts for insects by waiting on a post or low tree and flying out to capture them as they pass by. Drops to the ground to hunt for insects much more than other flycatchers. Male performs an up-down and zigzag courtship flight, showing off his long tail. Sometimes will end the flight with a reverse somersault. When not breeding, often seen in large flocks. Roosts communally, with up to 200 individuals. Closely related to kingbirds.

winter
p. 323

breeding

Black-bellied Plover
Pluvialis squatarola

YEAR-ROUND
MIGRATION

Size: 11–12" (28–30 cm)

Male: Striking black and white breeding plumage. Belly, breast, sides, face and neck are black. Cap, nape of neck, and belly near tail are white. Black legs and bill.

Female: less black on belly and breast than male

Juvenile: grayer than adults, with much less black

Nest: ground; male and female construct; 1 brood per year

Eggs: 3–4; pinkish or greenish with black-brown markings

Incubation: 26–27 days; male incubates during the day, female incubates at night

Fledging: 35–45 days; male feeds the young, and the young learn quickly to feed themselves

Migration: complete to non-migrator, to coastal Texas, Mexico, Central America and South America

Food: insects

Compare: Larger than the breeding Spotted Sandpiper (p. 173), which lacks the black belly. Look for Black-bellied's large black patch on the belly, face and chest, and a white cap.

Stan's Notes: Males perform a "butterfly" courtship flight to attract females. Female leaves male and young about 12 days after the eggs hatch. Breeds at age 3. A common year-round resident along the coast. Migrating birds arrive in Texas in July and August (fall migration) and leave in April. During flight, in any plumage, displays a white rump and stripe on wings with black axillaries (armpits). Often darts across the ground to grab an insect and run.

Black-necked Stilt

Himantopus mexicanus

YEAR-ROUND
SUMMER
MIGRATION

Size: 14" (36 cm)

Male: Black-and-white with ridiculously long red-to-pink legs. Upper parts of the head, neck and back are black. Lower parts are white. Long black bill.

Female: similar to male but browner on back

Juvenile: similar to female but brown instead of black

Nest: ground; female and male construct; 1 brood per year

Eggs: 3–5; off-white with dark markings

Incubation: 22–26 days; male incubates during the day, female incubates at night

Fledging: 28–32 days; female and male feed the young

Migration: complete to non-migrator in Texas

Food: aquatic insects

Compare: Outrageous length of the red-to-pink legs makes this shorebird hard to confuse with any other.

Stan's Notes: Seen year-round along the coast in Texas, it can be found along the East Coast and as far north as the Great Lakes. Nests alone or in small colonies in open areas. This very vocal bird of shallow marshes gives a "kek-kek-kek" call. Its legs are up to 10 inches (25 cm) long and may be the longest legs in the bird world in proportion to the body. Known to transport water with water-soaked belly feathers (belly-soaking) to cool eggs in hot weather. Aggressively defends its nest, eggs and young. Young leave the nest shortly after hatching.

female
p. 203

male

Bufflehead
Bucephala albeola

WINTER

Size: 13–15" (33–38 cm)

Male: A small, striking duck with white sides and a black back. Greenish-purple head, iridescent in bright sun, with a large white head patch.

Female: brownish-gray with a dark brown head and white cheek patch behind the eyes

Juvenile: similar to female

Nest: cavity; female lines an old woodpecker cavity; 1 brood per year

Eggs: 8–10; ivory-to-olive without markings

Incubation: 29–31 days; female incubates

Fledging: 50–55 days; female leads the young to food

Migration: complete, to Texas, Mexico, Central America

Food: aquatic insects, crustaceans, mollusks

Compare: Male Hooded Merganser (p. 87) is larger and has rust-brown sides. Look for the large white bonnet-like patch on a greenish-purple head to help identify the male Bufflehead.

Stan's Notes: A small, common diving duck, almost always seen in small groups or with other duck species on rivers, ponds and lakes. Nests in vacant woodpecker holes. When cavities in trees are scarce, known to use a burrow in an earthen bank or will use a nest box. Lines the cavity with fluffy down feathers. Unlike other ducks, the young stay in the nest for up to two days before they venture out with their mothers. The female is very territorial and remains with the same mate for many years.

female p. 225

male

WINTER

Lesser Scaup
Aythya affinis

Size: 16–17" (40–43 cm)

Male: Appears mostly black with bold white sides and a gray back. Chest and head look nearly black, but head appears purple with green highlights in direct sun. Bright-yellow eyes.

Female: overall brown with a dull-white patch at the base of a light-gray bill; yellow eyes

Juvenile: same as female

Nest: ground; female builds; 1 brood per year

Eggs: 8–14; olive-buff without markings

Incubation: 22–28 days; female incubates

Fledging: 45–50 days; female teaches the young to feed

Migration: complete, to Texas, Mexico, Central America and northern South America

Food: aquatic plants and insects

Compare: The male Ring-necked Duck (p. 89) has a bold white ring around its bill, a black back and lacks the bold white sides of the male Lesser Scaup. The male Blue-winged Teal (p. 217) is slightly smaller, with a white crescent on its bill. The white sides and gray back help identify the male Lesser Scaup.

Stan's Notes: A common diving duck. Often seen in large flocks on lakes and ponds. Submerges completely to feed on the bottom (unlike dabbling ducks, which tip forward to reach the bottom). The male leaves the female when she starts incubating eggs. Egg quantity (clutch size) increases with the female's age. Has an interesting babysitting arrangement: groups of young (crèches) are tended by one to three adult females.

female
p. 227

male

WINTER

Hooded Merganser
Lophodytes cucullatus

Size: 16–19" (40–48 cm)

Male: Black and white with rust-brown sides. Crest "hood" raises to show a large white patch on each side of the head. Long, thin, black bill.

Female: brown and rust with ragged, rust-red "hair" and a long, thin, brown bill

Juvenile: similar to female

Nest: cavity; female lines an old woodpecker cavity or a nest box near water; 1 brood per year

Eggs: 10–12; white without markings

Incubation: 32–33 days; female incubates

Fledging: 71 days; female feeds the young

Migration: complete, to the eastern half of Texas

Food: small fish, aquatic insects, crustaceans (especially crayfish)

Compare: Male Bufflehead (p. 83) is smaller than Hooded Merganser and has white sides. The male Wood Duck (p. 363) is similar in size, but has a green head. The white patch on the head and rust-brown sides distinguish the male Hoodie.

Stan's Notes: A small diving bird of shallow ponds, sloughs, lakes and rivers, usually in small groups. Quick, low flight across the water, with fast wingbeats. Male has a deep, rolling call. Female gives a hoarse quack. Nests in wooded areas. Female will lay some eggs in the nests of other Hooded Mergansers or Wood Ducks, resulting in 20–25 eggs in some nests. Rarely, she shares a nest, sitting with a Wood Duck.

female
p. 229

male

Ring-necked Duck

Aythya collaris

WINTER

Size: 16–19" (41–48 cm)

Male: Striking black duck with light-gray-to-white sides. Blue bill with a bold white ring and a thinner ring at the base. Peaked head with a sloped forehead.

Female: brown with darker-brown back and crown, light-brown sides, gray face, white eye-ring, white ring around the bill, and peaked head

Juvenile: similar to female

Nest: ground; female builds; 1 brood per year

Eggs: 8–10; olive-gray to brown without markings

Incubation: 26–27 days; female incubates

Fledging: 49–56 days; female teaches the young to feed

Migration: complete, to Texas, Mexico, Central America

Food: aquatic plants and insects

Compare: Similar size as male Lesser Scaup (p. 85), which has a gray back unlike the black back of male Ring-necked Duck. Look for the blue bill with a bold white ring to identify the male Ring-necked Duck.

Stan's Notes: A common winter duck throughout Texas. Usually in larger freshwater lakes rather than saltwater marshes, in small flocks or just pairs. Watch for this diving duck to dive underwater to forage for food. Springs up off the water to take flight. Flattens its crown when diving. Male gives a quick series of grating barks and grunts. Female gives high-pitched peeps. Named "Ring-necked" for its cinnamon collar, which is nearly impossible to see in the field. Also called Ring-billed Duck due to the white ring on its bill.

skimming

Black Skimmer
Rynchops niger

YEAR-ROUND

Size: 18" (45 cm); up to 3½' wingspan

Male: A striking black-and-white bird with black on top and white on bottom. Very distinct black-tipped red bill with lower bill longer than the upper. Red legs tuck up and out of sight when in flight.

Female: similar to male but smaller

Juvenile: similar to adults, spotty brown on top

Nest: ground; female and male construct; 1 brood per year

Eggs: 3–5; bluish white with brown markings

Incubation: 21–23 days; female and male incubate

Fledging: 23–25 days; female and male feed the young

Migration: non-migrator along coastal Texas

Food: small fish, shrimp

Compare: No other large black-and-white bird skims across the water like the Black Skimmer. In addition, no other bird has a lower bill that is longer than the upper bill.

Stan's Notes: Also called Scissorbill or Razorbill, referring to this bird's unusual long bill. Uses its unique bill while in flight to cut through the water to catch fish or shrimp close to the surface. Commonly feeds with several other skimmers. Often seen flying to and from nesting colony with fish in its bill. Nests in large colonies, often associated with terns. Found along the Gulf Coast.

winter

breeding

American Avocet
Recurvirostra americana

YEAR-ROUND
SUMMER
MIGRATION

Size: 18" (45 cm)

Male: Black-and-white back, with a white belly. A long, thin upturned bill and long gray legs. Rusty-red head and neck during breeding season, gray in winter.

Female: similar to male, more strongly upturned bill

Juvenile: similar to adults, slight wash of rusty red on the neck and head

Nest: ground; female and male construct; 1 brood per year

Eggs: 3–5; light olive with brown markings

Incubation: 22–29 days; female and male incubate

Fledging: 28–35 days; female and male feed young

Migration: partial migrator to non-migrator in Texas

Food: insects, crustaceans, aquatic vegetation, fruit

Compare: The White-faced Ibis (p. 267) is larger and has a down-curved bill. Look for the rusty-red head of breeding Avocet and the long upturned bill.

Stan's Notes: A handsome, long-legged bird that prefers shallow alkaline, saline or brackish water, it is well adapted to arid western U.S. conditions. Uses its upturned bill to sweep from side to side across mud bottoms in search of insects. Both the male and female have a brood patch to incubate eggs and brood their young. Nests in loose colonies of up to 20 pairs; all members defend against intruders together.

male

female

Pileated Woodpecker
Dryocopus pileatus

YEAR-ROUND

Size: 19" (48 cm)

Male: Crow-size woodpecker with a black back and bright-red forehead, crest and mustache. Long gray bill. White leading edge of wings flashes brightly during flight.

Female: same as male but with a black forehead; lacks a red mustache

Juvenile: similar to adults but duller and browner

Nest: cavity; male and female excavate; 1 brood per year

Eggs: 3–5; white without markings

Incubation: 15–18 days; female incubates during the day, male incubates at night

Fledging: 26–28 days; female and male feed the young

Migration: non-migrator

Food: insects; will come to suet and peanut feeders

Compare: The Red-headed Woodpecker (p. 71) is about half the size and has an all-red head. Look for the bright-red crest and exceptionally large size to identify the Pileated Woodpecker.

Stan's Notes: Our largest woodpecker. The common name comes from the Latin *pileatus*, which means "wearing a cap." A relatively shy bird that prefers large tracts of woodland. Drums on hollow branches, chimneys and so forth to announce its territory. Excavates oval holes up to several feet long in tree trunks, looking for insects to eat. Large wood chips lie on the ground by excavated trees. Favorite food is carpenter ants. Feeds regurgitated insects to its young. Young emerge from the nest looking just like the adults.

soaring

Osprey
Pandion haliaetus

YEAR-ROUND
MIGRATION

Size: 21–24" (53–61 cm); up to 5½' wingspan

Male: Large eagle-like bird with a white chest, belly and head. Dark eye line. Nearly black back. Black "wrist" marks on the wings. Dark bill.

Female: same as male but slightly larger and with a necklace of brown streaks

Juvenile: similar to adults, with a light-tan breast

Nest: platform on a raised wooden platform, man-made tower or tall dead tree; female and male build; 1 brood per year

Eggs: 2–4; white with brown markings

Incubation: 32–42 days; female and male incubate

Fledging: 48–58 days; male and female feed the young

Migration: complete, to coastal Texas, Mexico, Central America and South America

Food: fish

Compare: The juvenile Bald Eagle (p. 103) is brown with white speckles. The adult Bald Eagle has an all-white head and tail. Look for the white belly and dark eye line to identify the Osprey.

Stan's Notes: The only species in its family, and the only raptor that plunges into water feetfirst to catch fish. Always near water. Can hover for a few seconds before diving. Carries fish in a head-first position for better aerodynamics. Wings angle back in flight. Often harassed by Bald Eagles for its catch. Gives a high-pitched, whistle-like call, often calling in flight as a warning. Mates have a long-term pair bond. May not migrate to the same wintering grounds. Was nearly extinct but is now doing well.

soaring

juvenile

Crested Caracara
Caracara cheriway

YEAR-ROUND

Size: 22–25" (56–63 cm); up to 4¼' wingspan

Male: Black body and wings with a white chin, upper neck and wing tips. Large, obvious black crest. A long neck. Orange facial skin just behind a large gray bill. Long, strong yellow legs. White tail with a black terminal band, seen in flight.

Female: same as male, but slightly larger

Juvenile: similar to adult, but black areas are brown, and white areas are tan

Nest: platform; female builds; 1 brood per year

Eggs: 2–3; white or pinkish with brown markings

Incubation: 26–30 days; female and male incubate

Fledging: 40–60 days; female and male feed young

Migration: non-migrator; moves around to find food

Food: carrion, small mammals, insects, reptiles

Compare: Osprey (p. 97) is similar in size, but lacks the black belly and orange facial skin. Look for a bold black-and-white pattern and long yellow legs to help identify.

Stan's Notes: Largest member of the falcon family. Found in open savanna or desert scrub habitat, often near ranches. Feeds mainly on roadkill, often coursing (patrolling) at low elevations on roads at sunrise. Very different from all other raptors in North America, using its legs to stalk and chase prey such as mice. Often seen with vultures, and often in pairs. Glides on flat wings, unlike vultures in flight, which hold their wings upward in a semi-V shape. Roosts in trees at night. Facial skin can change color, usually to pale gray.

in flight

juvenile

YEAR-ROUND
SUMMER
MIGRATION

Black-crowned Night-Heron
Nycticorax nycticorax

Size: 22–27" (56–69 cm); up to 3½' wingspan

Male: A stocky, hunched and inactive heron with black back and crown, white belly and gray wings. Long dark bill and bright-red eyes. Short dull-yellow legs. Breeding adult has 2 long white plumes on crown.

Female: same as male

Juvenile: golden-brown head and back with white spots, streaked breast, yellow-orange eyes, brown bill

Nest: platform; female and male build; 1 brood per year

Eggs: 3–5; light blue without markings

Incubation: 24–26 days; female and male incubate

Fledging: 42–48 days; female and male feed the young

Migration: non-migrator to partial migrator in Texas

Food: fish, aquatic insects

Compare: Yellow-crowned Night-Heron (p. 343) is similar in size, but has a white cheek patch and lacks the Black-crowned's black back. A perching Great Blue Heron (p. 347) looks twice the size of a Black-crowned. Look for a short-necked heron with a black back and crown.

Stan's Notes: A very secretive bird, this heron is most active near dawn and dusk (crepuscular). It hunts alone, but it nests in small colonies. Roosts in trees during the day. Often squawks if disturbed from the daytime roost. Often seen being harassed by other herons during days. Stalks quiet backwaters in search of small fish and crabs.

soaring

juvenile

soaring
juvenile

Bald Eagle

Haliaeetus leucocephalus

YEAR-ROUND
WINTER

Size: 31–37" (79–94 cm); up to 7½' wingspan

Male: White head and tail contrast sharply with the dark-brown-to-black body and wings. Large, curved yellow bill and yellow feet.

Female: same as male but larger

Juvenile: dark brown with white speckles and spots on the body and wings; gray bill

Nest: massive platform, usually in a tree; female and male build; 1 brood per year

Eggs: 2–3; off-white without markings

Incubation: 34–36 days; female and male incubate

Fledging: 75–90 days; female and male feed the young

Migration: partial migrator to non-migrator in Texas

Food: fish, carrion, birds (mainly ducks)

Compare: The Golden Eagle (p. 269), Black Vulture (p. 51) and Turkey Vulture (p. 53) lack the white head and white tail of adult Bald Eagle. The juvenile Golden Eagle, with its white wrist marks and white base of tail, is similar to the juvenile Bald Eagle.

Stan's Notes: Nearly became extinct due to DDT poisoning and illegal killing. Returns to the same nest each year, adding more sticks and enlarging it to huge proportions, at times up to 1,000 pounds (450 kg). In their midair mating ritual, one eagle flips upside down and locks talons with another. Both tumble, then break apart to continue flight. Not uncommon for juveniles to perform this mating ritual even though they have not reached breeding age. Long-term pair bond but will switch mates when not successful at reproducing. Juveniles attain the white head and tail at 4–5 years of age.

female
p. 147

male

Indigo Bunting

Passerina cyanea

SUMMER MIGRATION

Size: 5½" (14 cm)

Male: Vibrant-blue finch-like bird. Dark markings scattered on wings and tail.

Female: light-brown with faint markings

Juvenile: similar to female

Nest: cup; female builds; 2 broods per year

Eggs: 3–4; pale blue without markings

Incubation: 12–13 days; female incubates

Fledging: 10–11 days; female feeds the young

Migration: complete, to Mexico, Central America and South America

Food: insects, seeds, fruit; will visit seed feeders

Compare: The male Eastern and Western Bluebird (pp. 111 and 113) are larger and have a rust-red chest. Male Mountain Bluebird (p. 109) has a thin black bill and white lower belly.

Stan's Notes: Seen along woodland edges and in parks and yards, feeding on insects. Comes to seed feeders early in spring, before insects are plentiful. Usually only the males are noticed. The male often sings from treetops to attract a mate. The female is quiet. Actually a gray bird, without blue pigment in its feathers: like Blue Jays and other blue birds, sunlight is refracted within the structure of the feathers, making them appear blue. Plumage is iridescent in direct sun, duller in shade. Molts in spring to acquire body feathers with gray tips, which quickly wear off, revealing the bright-blue plumage. Molts in fall and appears like the female during winter. Migrates at night in flocks of 5–10 birds. Males return before the females and juveniles, often to the nest site of the preceding year. Juveniles move to within a mile of their birth site.

female
p. 163

male

Blue Grosbeak
Passerina caerulea

SUMMER

Size: 7" (18 cm)

Male: Overall blue bird with 2 chestnut wing bars. Large gray-to-silver bill. Black around base of bill.

Female: overall brown with darker wings and tail, 2 tan wing bars, large gray-to-silver bill

Juvenile: similar to female

Nest: cup; female builds; 1–2 broods per year

Eggs: 3–6; pale blue without markings

Incubation: 11–12 days; female incubates

Fledging: 9–10 days; female and male feed the young

Migration: complete, to Mexico and Central America

Food: insects, seeds; will come to seed feeders

Compare: The more common male Indigo Bunting (p. 105) is very similar, but it is smaller and lacks wing bars. The male Eastern, Mountain and Western Bluebirds (pp. 111, 109 and 113) are the same size, but they lack the chestnut wing bars and oversized bill.

Stan's Notes: This grosbeak returns to Texas in early May. A bird of semi-open habitats such as overgrown fields, riversides, woodland edges and fencerows. Visits seed feeders, where it is often confused with male Indigo Buntings. Frequently seen twitching and spreading its tail. The first-year males show only some blue, obtaining the full complement of blue feathers in the second winter. It has expanded northward, and its overall populations have increased over the past 30–40 years.

male

female

Mountain Bluebird
Sialia currucoides

WINTER

Size: 7" (18 cm)

Male: Overall sky-blue bird with a darker blue head, back, wings and tail. White lower belly. Thin black bill.

Female: similar to male, but paler with a nearly gray head and chest and a whitish belly

Juvenile: similar to adult of the same sex

Nest: cavity, old woodpecker cavity, wooden nest box; female builds; 1–2 broods per year

Eggs: 4–6; pale blue without markings

Incubation: 13–14 days; female incubates

Fledging: 22–23 days; female and male feed young

Migration: complete, to parts of Texas, Mexico

Food: insects, fruit

Compare: Eastern and Western Bluebirds (pp. 111 and 113) are similar, but they are darker blue with a rusty-red chest. Male Blue Grosbeak (p. 107) is the same size, but it has chestnut wing bars and a large bill.

Stan's Notes: Common in open mountainous country. Main diet is insects. Often hovers just before diving to the ground to grab an insect. Due to conservation of suitable nesting sites (dead trees with cavities and man-made nest boxes), populations have increased over the past 30 years. Like other bluebirds, Mountain Bluebirds take well to nest boxes and tolerate close contact with people. Female sits on baby birds (brood) for up to six days after the eggs hatch. Young imprint on their first nest box or cavity and then choose a similar type of box or cavity throughout their life. Any open field is a good place to look for Mountain Bluebirds.

male

female

Eastern Bluebird
Sialia sialis

YEAR-ROUND WINTER

Size: 7" (18 cm)

Male: Sky-blue head, back and tail. Rust-red breast and white belly.

Female: grayer than male, with a faint rusty breast and faint blue wings and tail

Juvenile: similar to female but with spots on the breast and blue wing markings

Nest: cavity, vacant woodpecker cavity or nest box; female adds a soft lining; 2 broods per year

Eggs: 4–5; pale blue without markings

Incubation: 12–14 days; female incubates

Fledging: 15–18 days; male and female feed the young

Migration: complete to non-migrator in Texas

Food: insects, fruit; comes to shallow dishes with live or dead mealworms, and to suet feeders

Compare: Male Western Bluebird (p. 113) has a blue throat and is rusty red on flanks. The Mountain Bluebird (p. 109) and male Indigo Bunting (p. 105) lack a rusty-red chest. Blue Jay (p. 121) is much larger and has a crest. Look for the rusty breast to help identify the Eastern Bluebird.

Stan's Notes: Once nearly eliminated from Texas due to a lack of nest cavities. Thanks to people who installed thousands of nest boxes, bluebirds now thrive. Prefers open habitats, such as farm fields, pastures and roadsides, but also likes forest edges, parks and yards. Song is a distinctive "churlee chur chur-lee." A year-round resident that is joined by many northern migrants in winter. The rust-red breast is like that of the American Robin, its cousin.

male

female

Western Bluebird
Sialia mexicana

YEAR-ROUND
WINTER

Size: 7" (18 cm)

Male: Deep blue head, neck, throat, back, wings and tail. Rusty red chest and flanks.

Female: similar to male, only duller with a gray head

Juvenile: similar to female, with a speckled chest

Nest: cavity, old woodpecker cavity, wooden nest box; female builds; 1–2 broods per year

Eggs: 4–6; pale blue without markings

Incubation: 13–14 days; female incubates

Fledging: 22–23 days; female and male feed young

Migration: non-migrator to partial migrator in Texas

Food: insects, fruit

Compare: The male Eastern Bluebird (p. 111) looks very similar but lacks male Western's blue throat and rusty red on flanks. Mountain Bluebird (p. 109) and male Indigo Bunting (p. 105) are similar but lack the rusty-red breast. Male Blue Grosbeak (p. 107) is the same size but has chestnut wing bars and an oversized bill.

Stan's Notes: Found in a variety of habitats, from agricultural land to clear-cuts. Requires a cavity for nesting. Competes with starlings for nest cavities. Like the Mountain Bluebird, it uses nest boxes, which are responsible for the stable populations. Populations dropped during the mid-1900s but recovered due to the efforts of concerned people who put up nest boxes, providing much-needed habitats for nesting. A courting male will fly in front of the female, spread his wings and tail, and perch next to her. Often goes in and out of its nest box or cavity as if to say, "Look inside." Male may offer food to the female to establish a pair bond.

Barn Swallow

Hirundo rustica

SUMMER

Size: 7" (18 cm)

Male: Sleek swallow. Blue-black back, cinnamon belly and reddish-brown chin. White spots on a long, deeply forked tail.

Female: same as male but with a whitish belly

Juvenile: similar to adults, with a tan belly and chin, and shorter tail

Nest: cup; female and male build; 2 broods per year

Eggs: 4–5; white with brown markings

Incubation: 13–17 days; female incubates

Fledging: 18–23 days; female and male feed the young

Migration: complete, to South America

Food: insects (prefers beetles, wasps, flies)

Compare: The Cliff Swallow (p. 149) is smaller and lacks a distinctive, deeply forked tail. The Purple Martin (p. 117) is larger and has a dark-purple belly. The Chimney Swift (p. 131) has a narrow, pointed tail. Look for the deeply forked tail to identify the Barn Swallow.

Stan's Notes: Seen in wetlands, farms, suburban yards and parks. Of the seven swallow species regularly found in Texas, this is the only one with a deeply forked tail. Unlike other swallows, it rarely glides in flight. Usually flies low over land or water. Drinks as it flies, skimming water, or will sip water droplets on wet leaves. Bathes while flying through rain or sprinklers. Gives a twittering warble, followed by a mechanical sound. Builds a mud nest with up to 1,000 beak-loads of mud. Nests on barns and houses, under bridges and in other sheltered places. Often nests in colonies of 4–6 birds; sometimes nests alone.

male

female

Purple Martin
Progne subis

SUMMER

Size: 8½" (22 cm)

Male: Iridescent with a purple-to-black head, back and belly. Black wings and a notched black tail.

Female: grayish-purple head and back, darker wings and tail, whitish belly

Juvenile: same as female

Nest: cavity; female and male line the cavity of the house; 1 brood per year

Eggs: 4–5; white without markings

Incubation: 15–18 days; female incubates

Fledging: 26–30 days; male and female feed the young

Migration: complete, to South America

Food: insects

Compare: Usually seen only in groups. The male Purple Martin is the only swallow with a very dark-purplish belly.

Stan's Notes: The largest swallow species in North America. Once nested in tree cavities; now nests almost exclusively in man-made, apartment-style houses. The most successful colonies often nest in multiunit nest boxes within 100 feet (30 m) of a human dwelling near a lake. Main diet consists of dragonflies, not mosquitoes, as once thought. Gives a continuous stream of chirps, creaks and rattles, along with a shout-like "churrr" and chortle. Often drinks in flight, skimming water, and bathes in flight, flying through rain. Returns to the same nest site each year; the males arrive before the females and yearlings. The young leave to form new colonies. Large colonies gather in fall before migrating to South America.

YEAR-ROUND

Woodhouse's Scrub-Jay

Apelocoma woodhouseii

Size: 11" (28 cm)

Male: Blue head, wings, tail and breast band. Brownish patch on back. Dull white chin, breast and belly. Very long tail.

Female: same as male

Juvenile: similar to adult, overall gray with light-blue wings and tail

Nest: cup; female and male construct; 1 brood per year

Eggs: 3–6; pale green with red brown markings

Incubation: 15–17 days; female incubates

Fledging: 18–20 days; female and male feed young

Migration: non-migrator

Food: insects, seeds, fruit; comes to seed feeders

Compare: Blue Jay (p. 121) is similar in size, but has a black necklace and crest. Look for a brownish patch on the back and white chin to help identify the Woodhouse's Scrub-Jay.

Stan's Notes: A tame bird of urban areas that visits feeders. Forms a long-term pair bond, with the male feeding female before and during incubation. Young of a pair remain close by for up to a couple years, helping parents raise subsequent brothers and sisters. Caches food by burying it for later consumption. Likely serves as a major distributor of oaks and pines by not returning to eat the seeds it buried.

Blue Jay
Cyanocitta cristata

YEAR-ROUND

Size: 12" (30 cm)

Male: Bright light-blue-and-white bird with a black necklace and gray belly. Large crest moves up and down at will. White face, wing bars and tip of tail. Black tail bands.

Female: same as male

Juvenile: same as adult but duller

Nest: cup; female and male construct; 1–2 broods per year

Eggs: 4–5; green to blue with brown markings

Incubation: 16–18 days; female incubates

Fledging: 17–21 days; female and male feed the young

Migration: non-migrator to partial migrator; will move around to find an abundant food source

Food: insects, fruit, carrion, seeds, nuts; visits seed feeders, ground feeders with corn or peanuts

Compare: The Belted Kingfisher (p. 123) has a larger, more ragged crest. The Eastern Bluebird (p. 111) is much smaller and has a rust-red breast. Look for the large crest to help identify the Blue Jay.

Stan's Notes: Highly intelligent, solving problems, gathering food and communicating more than other birds. Loud and noisy; mimics other birds. Known as the alarm of the forest, screaming at intruders. Imitates hawk calls around feeders to scare off other birds. One of the few birds to cache food; can remember where it hid thousands of nuts. Carries food in a pouch under its tongue (sublingually). Eats eggs and young from other nests. Feathers lack blue pigment; refracted sunlight causes the blue appearance.

male

female

Belted Kingfisher

Megaceryle alcyon

YEAR-ROUND
WINTER

Size: 12–14" (30–36 cm)

Male: Blue with white belly, blue-gray chest band, and black wing tips. Ragged crest moves up and down at will. Large head. Long, thick, black bill. White spot by eyes. Red-brown eyes.

Female: same as male but with rusty flanks and a rusty chest band below the blue-gray band

Juvenile: similar to female

Nest: cavity; female and male excavate in a bank of a river, lake or cliff; 1 brood per year

Eggs: 6–7; white without markings

Incubation: 23–24 days; female and male incubate

Fledging: 23–24 days; female and male feed the young

Migration: complete to non-migrator in Texas

Food: small fish

Compare: The Blue Jay (p. 121) is lighter blue and has a plain gray chest and belly. Woodhouse's Scrub-Jay (p. 119) is smaller. The Belted Kingfisher is rarely found away from water.

Stan's Notes: Usually found at the bank of a river, lake or large stream. Perches on a branch near water, dives in headfirst to catch a small fish, then returns to the branch to feed. Parents drop dead fish into the water to teach their young to dive. Can't pass bones through its digestive tract; regurgitates bone pellets after meals. Gives a loud call that sounds like a machine gun. Mates know each other by their calls. Digs a tunnel up to 4 feet (1 m) long to a nest chamber. Small white patches on dark wing tips flash during flight.

Purple Gallinule
Porphyrio martinicus

SUMMER

Size: 13" (33 cm)

Male: A vibrant blue head, breast and belly with iridescent green back and wings. Yellow-tipped red bill. White undertail. Yellow legs.

Female: same as male

Juvenile: brown version of adult, bronze legs

Nest: ground; female and male build; 1–2 broods per year

Eggs: 6–8; brown with dark markings

Incubation: 22–25 days; female and male incubate

Fledging: 55–60 days; female and male feed the young

Migration: complete, to Central and South America

Food: insects, snails, seeds, berries, frogs

Compare: American Coot (p. 39) is similar in size but is black and lacks a yellow-tipped red bill. Common Gallinule (p. 37) is a similar size, but it has a white side stripe and lacks the green back. Look for a white undertail to help identify the Purple Gallinule.

Stan's Notes: This is one of the most dramatic-looking birds in Texas. Uses its extremely long toes to walk on floating vegetation in freshwater and saltwater marshes, where it hunts for grasshoppers and other insects, seeds and frogs. Family groups stay together; first brood sometimes helps raise the second. A summer resident in eastern Texas. Individuals are known to wander well north of the state.

non-breeding

breeding

molting
juvenile

white
juvenile

Little Blue Heron
Egretta caerulea

**YEAR-ROUND
SUMMER**

Size: 22–26" (56–66 cm)

Male: Dark slate-blue to purple nearly all year. Dull-green legs and feet. Black-tipped blue-gray bill. Breeding adult has a reddish-purple head and neck with several long plumes on the crown.

Female: same as male

Juvenile: pure white overall, yellowish legs and feet, black-tipped gray bill

Nest: platform; female and male build; 1 brood per year

Eggs: 2–6; light blue without markings

Incubation: 20–23 days; female and male incubate

Fledging: 42–49 days; female and male feed the young

Migration: complete to non-migrator, to coastal Texas, Mexico, Central America and South America

Food: fish, aquatic insects

Compare: Tricolored Heron (p. 129) has a white belly. Snowy Egret (p. 401) can be confused with a juvenile Little Blue, but Snowy has bright-yellow feet, black legs and a solid black bill.

Stan's Notes: A year-round coastal resident, although much less numerous in winter. Unusual because the young look completely different from adults. All-white young turn blotchy white the first year. By the second year they look like the adult birds. A very slow stalker of prey in freshwater lakes and rivers, saltwater marshes and wetlands. Nests in large colonies near saltwater sites.

breeding

non-breeding

Tricolored Heron
Egretta tricolor

YEAR-ROUND
MIGRATION

Size: 24–28" (60–71 cm)

Male: Dark-blue head, wings and back of neck. White belly and white stripe on underside of neck. Small brown patches at base of neck, with lighter brown on the lower back. Legs are yellow to pale green. Long, slender bill with a dark tip.

Female: same as male

Juvenile: similar to adult, chestnut-brown in place of dark-blue areas

Nest: platform; female and male build; 1 brood per year

Eggs: 3–6; light blue without markings

Incubation: 21–25 days; female and male incubate

Fledging: 32–35 days; female and male feed the young

Migration: non-migrator to partial migrator in Texas

Food: fish, aquatic insects

Compare: Great Blue Heron (p. 347) is much larger and lacks white undersides. The Little Blue Heron (p. 127) is slightly smaller and lacks the yellow bill and white belly.

Stan's Notes: A medium-sized heron characterized by its white undersides. Like other herons, numbers have declined due to habitat loss. To hunt, it stands still and waits. Will also chase small fish. A year-round resident, although less numerous in the winter. Seen mainly in saltwater marshes and estuaries, but also in freshwater marshes inland. In spring and summer, known to wander as far as Kansas. Colony nester with other herons, one adult always on duty at the nest. Was not hunted for plumes like other herons.

Chimney Swift
Chaetura pelagica

Size: 5" (13 cm)

Male: Nondescript, cigar-shaped bird, usually seen in flight. Long, thin, brown body. Pointed tail and head. Long, backswept wings, longer than the body.

Female: same as male

Juvenile: same as adult

Nest: half cup; female and male build; 1 brood per year

Eggs: 4–5; white without markings

Incubation: 19–21 days; female and male incubate

Fledging: 28–30 days; female and male feed the young

Migration: complete, to South America

Food: insects caught in midair

Compare: The Purple Martin (p. 117) is much larger and darker. The Barn Swallow (p. 115) has a deeply forked tail. Look for the cigar shape to identify the Chimney Swift in flight.

Stan's Notes: One of the fastest fliers in the bird world. Spends all day flying, rarely perching. Flies in groups, feeding on insects flying 100 feet (30 m) or higher up in the air. Often called a Flying Cigar due to its body shape, which is pointed at both ends. Drinks and bathes during flight, skimming water. Gives a unique in-flight twittering call, often heard before the bird is seen. Hundreds roost in large chimneys, giving it the common name. Builds its nest with tiny twigs, cementing it with saliva and attaching it to the inside of a chimney or a hollow tree. Usually only one nest per chimney.

Chipping Sparrow
Spizella passerina

YEAR-ROUND
MIGRATION
WINTER

Size: 5" (13 cm)

Male: Small gray-brown sparrow with clear-gray chest. Rusty crown. White eyebrows and thin black eye line. Thin gray-black bill. Two faint wing bars.

Female: same as male

Juvenile: similar to adults, with streaking on the chest; lacks a rusty crown

Nest: cup; female builds; 2 broods per year

Eggs: 3–5; blue-green with brown markings

Incubation: 11–14 days; female incubates

Fledging: 10–12 days; female and male feed the young

Migration: complete to non-migrator in Texas

Food: insects, seeds; will come to ground feeders

Compare: The Lark Sparrow (p. 159) is larger and has a white chest and central spot. Song Sparrow (p. 151) and female House Finch (p. 137) have heavily streaked chests. Look for the rusty crown and black eye line to help identify the Chipping Sparrow.

Stan's Notes: A common garden or yard bird, often seen feeding on dropped seeds beneath feeders. Gathers in large family groups to feed in preparation for migration. Migrates at night in flocks of 20–30 birds. The common name comes from the male's fast "chip" call. Often is just called Chippy. Builds nest low in dense shrubs and almost always lines it with animal hair. Comfortable with people, allowing you to approach closely before it flies away.

133

Pine Siskin
Spinus pinus

WINTER

Size: 5" (13 cm)

Male: Small brown finch with heavy streaking on the back, breast and belly. Yellow wing bars. Yellow at the base of tail. Thin bill.

Female: similar to male, with less yellow

Juvenile: similar to adult, with a light-yellow tinge over the breast and chin

Nest: cup; female builds; 2 broods

Eggs: 3–4; greenish blue with brown markings

Incubation: 12–13 days; female incubates

Fledging: 14–15 days; female and male feed the young

Migration: irruptive; moves around the United States in search of food

Food: seeds, insects; will come to seed feeders

Compare: Female House Finch (p. 137) lacks any yellow. The female American Goldfinch (p. 415) has white wing bars. Look for the yellow wing bars to identify the Pine Siskin.

Stan's Notes: Usually considered a winter finch. Conspicuous in some winters, rare in others. Seen in flocks of up to 20 birds, often with other finch species. Gathers in flocks and moves around, visiting feeders. Will come to thistle feeders. Gives a series of high-pitched, wheezy calls. Also gives a wheezing twitter. Breeds in small groups. Builds nest toward the end of coniferous branches, where needles are dense, helping to conceal. Nests are often only a few feet apart. Male feeds the female during incubation. Juveniles lose the yellow tint by late summer of their first year.

male
p. 379

female

House Finch
Haemorhous mexicanus

YEAR-ROUND

Size: 5" (13 cm)

Female: Plain brown with heavy streaking on a white chest.

Male: red-to-orange face, throat, chest and rump; streaked belly and wings; brown cap; brown marking behind the eyes

Juvenile: similar to female

Nest: cup, occasionally in a cavity; female builds; 2 broods per year

Eggs: 4–5; pale blue, lightly marked

Incubation: 12–14 days; female incubates

Fledging: 15–19 days; female and male feed the young

Migration: non-migrator; will move around to find food

Food: seeds, fruit, leaf buds; visits seed feeders and feeders that offer grape jelly

Compare: Pine Siskin (p. 135) is similar but has yellow wing bars and a smaller bill. The female American Goldfinch (p. 415) has a clear chest. Look for the heavily streaked chest to help identify the female House Finch.

Stan's Notes: Can be a common bird at your feeders. A very social bird, visiting feeders in small flocks. Likes to nest in hanging flower baskets. Male sings a loud, cheerful warbling song. A native finch to Texas and was introduced to Long Island, New York, from the western U.S. in the 1940s. Now found throughout the country. Suffers from a disease that causes the eyes to crust, resulting in blindness and death.

House Wren
Troglodytes aedon

MIGRATION
WINTER

Size: 5" (13 cm)

Male: All-brown bird with lighter-brown markings on the wings and tail. Slightly curved brown bill. Often holds tail upward.

Female: same as male

Juvenile: same as adult

Nest: cavity; female and male line just about any nest cavity; 2 broods per year

Eggs: 4–6; tan with brown markings

Incubation: 10–13 days; female and male incubate

Fledging: 12–15 days; female and male feed the young

Migration: complete, to southern Texas, Mexico

Food: insects, spiders, snails

Compare: Carolina Wren (p. 141) and Bewick's Wren (p. 143) are slightly larger and have prominent eyebrows. Look for House Wren's long curved bill and long upturned tail to differentiate it from sparrows.

Stan's Notes: A prolific songster. During the mating season, sings from dawn to dusk. Seen in brushy yards, parks and woodlands and along forest edges. Easily attracted to a nest box. In spring, the male chooses several prospective nesting cavities and places a few small twigs in each. The female inspects all of them and finishes constructing the nest in the cavity of her choice. She fills the cavity with short twigs and then lines a small depression at the back with pine needles and grass. She often has trouble fitting longer twigs through the entrance hole and tries many different directions and approaches until she is successful.

Carolina Wren

Thryothorus ludovicianus

YEAR-ROUND

Size: 5½" (14 cm)

Male: Rusty-brown head and back with an orange-yellow chest and belly. White throat and a prominent white eye stripe. Short, stubby tail, often cocked up.

Female: same as male

Juvenile: same as adults

Nest: cavity; female and male build; 2 broods per year, sometimes 3

Eggs: 4–6; white, sometimes pink or creamy, with brown markings

Incubation: 12–14 days; female incubates

Fledging: 12–14 days; female and male feed the young

Migration: non-migrator

Food: insects, fruit, few seeds; visits suet feeders

Compare: House Wren (p. 139) is darker brown and lacks the bold white eye stripe. Bewick's Wren (p. 143) is similar but lacks Carolina Wren's orange-yellow chest and belly.

Stan's Notes: A year-round resident in eastern and central Texas. Mates are long-term, staying together throughout the year in permanent territories. Sings year-round. The male is known to sing up to 40 song types, singing one song repeatedly before switching to another. The female also sings, resulting in duets. The male often takes over feeding the first brood while the female renests. Nests in birdhouses and in unusual places like mailboxes, bumpers or broken taillights of vehicles, or nearly any other cavity. Found in brushy yards or woodlands. Can be attracted to feeders with mealworms.

Bewick's Wren
Thryomanes bewickii

YEAR-ROUND

Size: 5½" (14 cm)

Male: Brown cap, back, wings and tail. Gray chest and belly. White chin and eyebrows. Long tail with white spots on edges is cocked and flits sideways. Pointed down-curved bill.

Female: same as male

Juvenile: similar to adult

Nest: cavity; female and male build nest in woodpecker hole or nest box; 2–3 broods a year

Eggs: 4–8; white with brown markings

Incubation: 12–14 days; female incubates

Fledging: 10–14 days; female and male feed young

Migration: non-migrator

Food: insects, seeds

Compare: The House Wren (p. 139) is slightly smaller and lacks the obvious white eyebrow marks and white spots on tail. Similar to Carolina Wren (p. 141), but the Bewick's Wren has a gray chest.

Stan's Notes: A common wren of backyards and gardens. Insects make up 97 percent of its diet, with plant seeds composing the rest. Competes with House Wrens for nesting cavities. Male will choose nesting cavities and start to build nests using small uniform-sized sticks. Female will make the final selection of a nest site and finish building. Begins breeding in March and April. Has 2–3 broods per year. Male feeds female while she incubates. Average size territory per pair is 5 acres (2 ha), which they defend all year long. The brown (Eastern) and grayish brown (Western) Bewick's both occur in Texas. Map reflects the combined range.

male
p. 283

female

pink-sided

Oregon
female

Dark-eyed Junco

Junco hyemalis

WINTER

Size: 5½" (14 cm)

Female: A plump, dark-eyed bird with a tan-to-brown chest, head and back. White belly. Ivory-to-pink bill. White outer tail feathers appear like a white V in flight.

Male: round bird with gray plumage

Juvenile: similar to female, with streaking on the breast and head

Nest: cup; female and male build; 2 broods per year

Eggs: 3–5; white with reddish-brown markings

Incubation: 12–13 days; female incubates

Fledging: 10–13 days; male and female feed the young

Migration: complete, to Texas

Food: seeds, insects; visits ground and seed feeders

Compare: Rarely confused with any other bird. Look for the ivory-to-pink bill and small flocks feeding beneath seed feeders to help identify the female Dark-eyed Junco.

Stan's Notes: Adheres to a rigid social hierarchy, with dominant birds chasing the less dominant birds. Look for the white outer tail feathers flashing in flight. Often seen in small flocks on the ground, where it uses its feet to simultaneously "double-scratch" to expose seeds and insects. Eats many weed seeds. Nests in a wide variety of wooded habitats in April and May. Doesn't nest in Texas. Several subspecies of Dark-eyed Junco were previously considered to be separate species (see lower insets).

female

male
p. 105

Indigo Bunting
Passerina cyanea

SUMMER
MIGRATION

Size: 5½" (14 cm)

Female: Light-brown, finch-like bird. Faint streaking on a light-tan chest. Wings have a very faint blue cast and indistinct wing bars.

Male: vibrant blue with scattered dark markings on wings and tail

Juvenile: similar to female

Nest: cup; female builds; 2 broods per year

Eggs: 3–4; pale blue without markings

Incubation: 12–13 days; female incubates

Fledging: 10–11 days; female feeds the young

Migration: complete, to Mexico, Central America and South America

Food: insects, seeds, fruit; will visit seed feeders

Compare: Female Blue Grosbeak (p. 163) is larger and has 2 tan wing bars. The female House Finch (p. 137) has a heavily streaked chest. Female American Goldfinch (p. 415) has white wing bars. Look for the faint blue cast on the wings to help identify the female Indigo Bunting.

Stan's Notes: Seen along woodland edges and in parks and yards, feeding on insects. Comes to seed feeders early in spring, before insects are plentiful. Secretive, plain and quiet; usually only the males are noticed. The male often sings from treetops to attract a mate. Migrates at night in flocks of 5–10 birds. Males return before the females and juveniles, often to the nest site of the preceding year. Juveniles move to within a mile of their birth site.

Cliff Swallow
Petrochelidon pyrrhonota

SUMMER

Size: 5½" (14 cm)

Male: Uniquely patterned swallow with a dark back, wings and cap. Distinctive tan-to-rust rump, cheeks and forehead.

Female: same as male

Juvenile: similar to adult, lacks distinct patterning

Nest: gourd-shaped, made of mud; male and female build; 1–2 broods per year

Eggs: 4–6; pale white with brown markings

Incubation: 14–16 days; male and female incubate

Fledging: 21–24 days; female and male feed young

Migration: complete, to South America

Food: insects

Compare: Smaller than Barn Swallow (p. 115), which has a distinctive, deeply forked tail and blue back and wings.

Stan's Notes: Common and widespread in Texas during summer. Common around bridges (especially bridges over water) and rural housing (especially in open country near cliffs). Builds a gourd-shaped nest with a funnel-like entrance pointing down. A colony nester, with many nests lined up beneath building eaves or cliff overhangs. Will carry balls of mud up to a mile to construct its nest. Many in the colony return to the same nest site each year. Not unusual to have two broods per season. If the number of nests underneath eaves becomes a problem, wait until the young have left the nests to hose off the mud.

Song Sparrow
Melospiza melodia

WINTER

Size: 5–6" (13–15 cm)

Male: Common brown sparrow with heavy dark streaks on the chest coalescing into a central dark spot.

Female: same as male

Juvenile: similar to adults, with a finely streaked chest; lacks a central dark spot

Nest: cup; female builds; 2 broods per year

Eggs: 3–4; blue to green, with red-brown markings

Incubation: 12–14 days; female incubates

Fledging: 9–12 days; female and male feed the young

Migration: complete, to Texas

Food: insects, seeds; only rarely comes to ground feeders with seeds

Compare: Similar to other brown sparrows. Look for the heavily streaked chest with a central dark spot to help identify the Song Sparrow.

Stan's Notes: There are many subspecies of this bird, but the dark spot in the center of the chest appears in every variety. A constant songster, repeating its loud, clear song every few minutes. The song varies from region to region but has the same basic structure. Sings from thick shrubs to defend a small territory, beginning with three notes and finishing up with a trill. A ground feeder, it will "double-scratch" with both feet at the same time to expose seeds. When the female builds a new nest for a second brood, the male often takes over feeding the first brood. Unlike many other sparrow species, Song Sparrows rarely flock together. A common host of the Brown-headed Cowbird.

male

female

House Sparrow
Passer domesticus

YEAR-ROUND

Size: 6" (15 cm)

Male: Brown back with a gray belly and cap. Large black patch extending from the throat to the chest (bib). One white wing bar.

Female: slightly smaller than the male; light brown with light eyebrows; lacks a bib and white wing bar

Juvenile: similar to female

Nest: cavity; female and male build a domed cup nest within; 2–3 broods per year

Eggs: 4–6; white with brown markings

Incubation: 10–12 days; female incubates

Fledging: 14–17 days; female and male feed the young

Migration: non-migrator; moves around to find food

Food: seeds, insects, fruit; comes to seed feeders

Compare: Chipping Sparrow (p. 133) has a rusty crown. Look for the black bib to identify the male House Sparrow and the clear breast to help identify the female.

Stan's Notes: One of the first birdsongs heard in cities in spring. A familiar city bird, nearly always in small flocks. Also found on farms. Introduced in 1850 from Europe to Central Park in New York. Now seen throughout North America. Related to old-world sparrows; not a relative of any sparrows in the U.S. An aggressive bird that will kill young birds in order to take over the nest cavity. Uses dried grass and small scraps of plastic, paper and other materials to build an oversize, domed nest in the cavity.

winter p. 293

breeding

Least Sandpiper
Calidris minutilla

YEAR-ROUND
MIGRATION
WINTER

Size: 6" (15 cm)

Male: Breeding plumage has a golden-brown head and back and a white belly. Dull-yellow legs. White eyebrows and a short, down-curved black bill.

Female: same as male

Juvenile: similar to winter adult but buff-brown and lacks the breast band

Nest: ground; male and female construct; 1 brood per year

Eggs: 3–4; olive with dark markings

Incubation: 19–23 days; male and female incubate

Fledging: 25–28 days; male and female feed the young

Migration: complete to non-migrator, to Texas, Mexico and Central America

Food: aquatic and terrestrial insects, seeds

Compare: The smallest of sandpipers. Look for Least Sandpiper's yellow legs to differentiate it from other tiny sandpipers. The short, thin down-curved bill also helps to identify.

Stan's Notes: Winters in southern coastal states from the Carolinas to California. This is a tiny, tame sandpiper that can be approached without scaring it. It is the smallest of peeps (sandpipers), nesting on the tundra in northern regions of Canada and Alaska. Prefers the grassy flats of saltwater and freshwater ponds. Its yellow legs can be hard to see in water, poor light or when covered with mud. Most other small shorebirds have black legs and feet.

male
p. 59

female

non-breeding
male

Lark Bunting
Calamospiza melanocorys

SUMMER
WINTER

Size: 6½" (16 cm)

Female: Brown bird with heavily streaked chest and a white belly. Black vertical line on each side of white chin. May have a central dark spot on the chest. Faint white eyebrows.

Male: black bird with a large broad head, white wing patches and large bluish-gray bill

Juvenile: similar to adult of the same sex

Nest: cup; female builds; 1–2 broods per year

Eggs: 4–6; pale blue with markings

Incubation: 11–13 days; female and male incubate

Fledging: 8–12 days; female and male feed young

Migration: complete, to most of Texas, Mexico

Food: insects, seeds

Compare: Appears similar to open-country sparrows. The female Red-winged Blackbird (p. 181) lacks the white belly and chin.

Stan's Notes: Common in the dry plains and sagebrush regions of the state. Has short rounded wings. Flying with shallow wingbeats, the male flashes white wing patches. Male takes to air to display to female, setting its wings in a V position and floating back, rocking like a butterfly, singing a most amazing song. Song is like the song of Old World larks, hence the common name. Will flock in fall with hundreds, if not thousands, of other Lark Buntings for migration.

Lark Sparrow
Chondestes grammacus

YEAR-ROUND
SUMMER

Size: 6½" (16 cm)

Male: All-brown bird with unique rust-red, white and black head pattern. A white breast with a central black spot. Gray rump and white edges to gray tail, as seen in flight.

Female: same as male

Juvenile: similar to adult, no rust-red on head

Nest: cup, on the ground; female builds; 1 brood per year

Eggs: 3–6; pale white with brown markings

Incubation: 10–12 days; male and female incubate

Fledging: 10–12 days; female and male feed young

Migration: non-migrator to complete in Texas

Food: seeds, insects

Compare: Larger than Chipping Sparrow (p. 133), which has a similar rusty color on head but lacks Lark Sparrow's white breast and central spot.

Stan's Notes: One of the larger sparrow species and one of the best songsters, also well known for its courtship strutting, chasing and lark-like flight pattern (rapid wingbeats with tail spread). A bird of open fields, pastures and prairies, found almost anywhere. Very common during migration, when large flocks congregate. Will use nest for several years if first brood is successful.

white-striped

tan-striped

White-throated Sparrow
Zonotrichia albicollis

MIGRATION
WINTER

Size: 6–7" (15–18 cm)

Male: Brown with a gray or tan chest and belly. White or tan throat patch and eyebrows. Bold striping on the head. Small yellow spot in the space between the eye and bill, called the lore.

Female: same as male

Juvenile: similar to adults, with a heavily streaked chest and a gray throat and eyebrows

Nest: cup; female builds; 1 brood per year

Eggs: 4–6; green to blue, or cream-white with red-brown markings

Incubation: 11–14 days; female incubates

Fledging: 10–12 days; female and male feed the young

Migration: complete, to Texas and Mexico

Food: insects, seeds, fruit; visits ground feeders

Compare: Song Sparrow (p. 151) has a central spot on the breast and lacks a striped pattern on the head.

Stan's Notes: Two color variations (polymorphic): white-striped and tan-striped. Studies indicate that the white-striped adults tend to mate with the tan-striped birds; it's not clear why. Known for its wonderful song; it sings all year and can even be heard at night. White- and tan-striped males and white-striped females sing, but tan-striped females do not. Builds nest on the ground under small trees in bogs and coniferous forests. Often associated with other sparrows in winter. Feeds on the ground under feeders. Immature and first-year females tend to winter farther south than adults. Doesn't nest in Texas.

male
p. 107

female

Blue Grosbeak
Passerina caerulea

SUMMER

Size: 7" (18 cm)

Female: Overall brown with darker wings and tail. Two tan wing bars. Large gray-to-silver bill.

Male: blue bird with 2 chestnut wing bars; large gray-to-silver bill; black around base of bill

Juvenile: similar to female

Nest: cup; female builds; 1–2 broods per year

Eggs: 3–6; pale blue without markings

Incubation: 11–12 days; female incubates

Fledging: 9–10 days; female and male feed the young

Migration: complete, to Mexico and Central America

Food: insects, seeds; will come to seed feeders

Compare: The female Indigo Bunting (p. 147) is very similar, but it lacks the tan wing bars and is lighter in color overall.

Stan's Notes: This grosbeak returns to Texas by early May. A bird of semi-open habitats such as overgrown fields, riversides, woodland edges and fencerows. Visits seed feeders, where it can be confused with female Indigo Buntings. Often seen twitching and spreading its tail. The first-year males show only some blue, obtaining the full complement of blue feathers in the second winter. It has expanded northward, and its overall populations have increased over the past 30–40 years.

male
p. 25

female

Bronzed
Cowbird

Brown-headed Cowbird

Molothrus ater

YEAR-ROUND

Size: 7½" (19 cm)

Female: Dull brown with no obvious markings. Pointed, sharp, gray bill. Dark eyes.

Male: glossy black with a chocolate-brown head

Juvenile: similar to female but with dull-gray plumage and a streaked chest

Nest: no nest; lays eggs in the nests of other birds

Eggs: 5–7; white with brown markings

Incubation: 10–13 days; host bird incubates the eggs

Fledging: 10–11 days; host birds feed the young

Migration: non-migrator in Texas

Food: insects, seeds; will come to seed feeders

Compare: The female Red-winged Blackbird (p. 181) has white eyebrows and heavy streaking. The female Indigo Bunting (p. 147) has faint blue on its wings. The pointed gray bill helps to identify the female Brown-headed Cowbird.

Stan's Notes: Cowbirds are members of the blackbird family. One of two species of parasitic bird in Texas. The Bronzed Cowbird (see inset) is easily identified by its bright-red eyes. Brood parasites lay their eggs in the nests of other birds, leaving the host birds to raise their young. Cowbirds are known to have laid their eggs in the nests of over 200 species of birds. While some birds reject cowbird eggs, most incubate them and raise the young, even to the exclusion of their own. Look for warblers and other birds feeding young birds twice their own size. Named "Cowbird" for its habit of following bison and cattle herds to feed on insects flushed up by the animals.

1 year
old

Cedar Waxwing
Bombycilla cedrorum

WINTER

Size: 7½" (19 cm)

Male: Sleek-looking, gray-to-brown bird. Pointed crest, bandit-like mask and light-yellow belly. Bold-yellow tip of tail. Red wing tips look like they were dipped in red wax.

Female: same as male

Juvenile: grayish with a heavily streaked breast; lacks the sleek look, black mask and red wing tips

Nest: cup; female and male construct; 1 brood per year, occasionally 2

Eggs: 4–6; pale blue with brown markings

Incubation: 10–12 days; female incubates

Fledging: 14–18 days; female and male feed the young

Migration: complete to partial migrator; moves to Texas to find food

Food: cedar cones, fruit, insects

Compare: The female Northern Cardinal (p. 177) has a large red bill. Look for the red wing tips, yellow-tipped tail and black mask to identify the Cedar Waxwing.

Stan's Notes: The name is derived from its red, wax-like wing tips and preference for the small, berry-like cones of the cedar. Seen in flocks, moving around from area to area looking for berries. Feeds on insects during summer, before berries are abundant. Wanders during winter, searching for food supplies. Spends most of its time at the top of tall trees. Listen for the high-pitched "sreee" whistling sound it constantly makes while perched or in flight. Obtains the mask after the first year and red wing tips after the second year. Doesn't nest in Texas.

female

male

Horned Lark
Eremophila alpestris

YEAR-ROUND

Size: 7–8" (18–20 cm)

Male: Tan to brown with black markings on the face. Black necklace and bill. Pale-yellow chin. Two tiny feather "horns" on the top of the head, sometimes hard to see. Dark tail with white outer tail feathers, seen in flight.

Female: duller than male; less noticeable "horns"

Juvenile: lacks a yellow chin and black markings; does not develop "horns" until the second year

Nest: ground; female builds; 2–3 broods per year

Eggs: 3–4; gray with brown markings

Incubation: 11–12 days; female incubates

Fledging: 9–12 days; female and male feed the young

Migration: non-migrator in Texas

Food: seeds, insects

Compare: The Meadowlark (p. 439) has a yellow breast and belly. Look for the black markings by the eyes and the black necklace to identify the Horned Lark.

Stan's Notes: The only true lark native to North America. A bird of open ground. Common in rural areas; often seen in large flocks. The population increased in North America over the past century as more land was cleared for farming. Male performs a fluttering courtship flight high in the air while singing a high-pitched song. Female performs a fluttering distraction display when the nest is disturbed. Starts breeding early in the year. Able to renest about a week after the brood fledges. Moves around in winter to find food. "Lark" comes from the Middle English *laverock*, or "a lark."

male
p. 377

female

Black-headed Grosbeak
Pheucticus melanocephalus

SUMMER
MIGRATION

Size: 8" (20 cm)

Female: Appears like an overgrown sparrow. Overall brown with a lighter breast and belly. Large two-toned bill. Prominent white eyebrows. Yellow wing linings, as seen in flight.

Male: burnt-orange chest, neck and rump, black head, tail and wings with irregular-shaped white wing patches, large bill with upper bill darker than lower

Juvenile: similar to adult of the same sex

Nest: cup; female builds; 1 brood per year

Eggs: 3–4; pale green or bluish, brown markings

Incubation: 11–13 days; female and male incubate

Fledging: 11–13 days; female and male feed young

Migration: complete, to Mexico

Food: seeds, insects, fruit; comes to seed feeders

Compare: Female House Finch (p. 137) is smaller, has more streaking on the chest and the bill isn't as large. Look for female Grosbeak's unusual bicolored bill.

Stan's Notes: A cosmopolitan bird that nests in a wide variety of habitats. Both the male and female sing and will aggressively defend the nest against intruders. Song is very similar to American Robin's (p. 315), making it hard to tell them apart by song. Populations increasing in Texas and across the U.S.

winter

breeding

Spotted Sandpiper
Actitis macularius

MIGRATION
WINTER

Size: 8" (20 cm)

Male: Olive-brown back with black spots on a white chest and belly. White line over eyes. Long, dull-yellow legs. Long bill. Winter plumage lacks spots on the chest and belly.

Female: same as male

Juvenile: similar to winter plumage, with a darker bill

Nest: ground; male builds; 2 broods per year

Eggs: 3–4; brownish with brown markings

Incubation: 20–24 days; male incubates

Fledging: 17–21 days; male feeds the young

Migration: complete migrator, to the southern half of Texas; Mexico, Central and South America

Food: aquatic insects

Compare: Killdeer (p. 193) has 2 black neck bands. Look for the black spots on the chest and belly and the bobbing tail to help identify the breeding Spotted Sandpiper.

Stan's Notes: This is one of the more common sandpipers. Seen along the shorelines of large ponds, lakes and rivers. One of the few shorebirds that will dive underwater when pursued. Able to fly straight up out of the water. Holds wings in a cup-like arc in flight, rarely lifting them above a horizontal plane. Walks as if delicately balanced. When standing, constantly bobs its tail. Gives a rapid series of "weet-weet-weet" calls when frightened and flying away. Female mates with multiple males and lays eggs in up to five nests. Male does all of the nest building, incubating and childcare without any help from the female.

winter
p. 305

breeding

Sanderling
Calidris alba

YEAR-ROUND
MIGRATION

Size:	8" (20 cm)
Male:	Breeding adult (April to August) has a rusty head, chest and back with white belly. Black legs and bill.
Female:	same as male
Juvenile:	spotty black on the head and back, a white belly, black legs and bill
Nest:	ground; male builds; 1–2 broods per year
Eggs:	3–4; greenish olive with brown markings
Incubation:	24–30 days; male and female incubate
Fledging:	16–17 days; female and male feed the young
Migration:	complete to non-migrator, to coastal Texas, Mexico, Central America and South America
Food:	insects
Compare:	Spotted Sandpiper (p. 173) is the same size as Sanderling, but the breeding Spotted Sandpiper has black spots on its chest.

Stan's Notes: One of the most common shorebirds in Texas, but mostly seen in its gray winter plumage from August to April. Can be seen in groups on sandy beaches, running out with each retreating wave to feed. Look for a flash of white on the wings when it is in flight. Sometimes a female will mate with several males (polyandry), which results in males and the female incubating separate nests. Both sexes perform a distraction display if threatened. Nests on the Arctic tundra. Rests by standing on one leg (see inset) and tucking the other leg into its belly feathers. Often hops away on one leg, moving away from pedestrians on the beach. Surveys show a greater than 80 percent decline in numbers since the 1970s.

male
p. 385

female

juvenile

Northern Cardinal
Cardinalis cardinalis

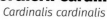

YEAR-ROUND

Size: 8–9" (20–23 cm)

Female: Buff-brown with red tinges on the crest and wings. Black mask and a large reddish bill.

Male: red with a large crest and bill and a black mask extending from the face to the throat

Juvenile: same as female but with a blackish-gray bill

Nest: cup; female builds; 2–3 broods per year

Eggs: 3–4; bluish white with brown markings

Incubation: 12–13 days; female and male incubate

Fledging: 9–10 days; female and male feed the young

Migration: non-migrator

Food: seeds, insects, fruit; comes to seed feeders

Compare: The Cedar Waxwing (p. 167) has a small dark bill. The juvenile Northern Cardinal (bottom inset) looks like the adult female but with a dark bill. Look for the reddish bill to identify the female Northern Cardinal.

Stan's Notes: A familiar backyard bird. Seen in a variety of habitats, including parks. Usually likes thick vegetation. One of the few species in which both females and males sing. Can be heard all year. Listen for its "whata-cheer-cheer-cheer" territorial call in spring. Watch for a male feeding a female during courtship. The male also feeds the young of the first brood while the female builds a second nest. Territorial in spring, fighting its own reflection in a window or other reflective surface. Non-territorial in winter, gathering in small flocks of up to 20 birds. Makes short flights from cover to cover, often landing on the ground. *Cardinalis* denotes importance, as represented by the red priestly garments of Catholic cardinals.

Cactus Wren

Campylorhynchus brunneicapillus

YEAR-ROUND

Size: 8½" (22 cm)

Male: Large round-bodied wren with a chestnut-brown crown and a long tail. Many dark spots on upper breast to throat, often forming a central dark patch. Bold white eyebrows. Large, slightly downward-curving bill.

Female: same as male

Juvenile: similar to adult, shorter bill, lacks a spotty dark patch on breast

Nest: covered cup, domed or ball-shaped; female and male build; 2–3 broods per year

Eggs: 3–4; pale white to pink with brown marks

Incubation: 14–16 days; female incubates

Fledging: 19–23 days; female and male feed young

Migration: non-migrator

Food: insects, fruit, seeds; comes to seed feeders and water elements

Compare: The Curve-billed Thrasher (p. 319) has a longer bill. Look for the Cactus Wren's prominent white eyebrows to help identify.

Stan's Notes: Our largest wren. Backyard bird with a loud "krr-krr-krr-krr-krr" or "cha-cha-cha-cha" call. Male crouches, extends wings, fans tail and growls to female during courtship. Pairs stay together all year, defending territory. Builds a large nest usually in cholla or other cactus, lining the chamber with grasses and feathers. Male builds another nest while female incubates first clutch of eggs. After the last brood fledges, roosts in nest during non-breeding season.

male
p. 31

female

Red-winged Blackbird
Agelaius phoeniceus

YEAR-ROUND

Size: 8½" (22 cm)

Female: Heavily streaked brown body. Pointed brown bill and white eyebrows.

Male: jet black with red-and-yellow shoulder patches (epaulets) and a pointed black bill

Juvenile: same as female

Nest: cup; female builds; 2–3 broods per year

Eggs: 3–4; bluish green with brown markings

Incubation: 10–12 days; female incubates

Fledging: 11–14 days; female and male feed the young

Migration: non-migrator to partial migrator

Food: seeds, insects; visits seed and suet feeders

Compare: Female Brown-headed Cowbird (p. 165) is smaller and female Yellow-headed Blackbird (p. 191) is larger, both of which lack white eyebrows and streaks on chest. Look for white eyebrows and heavy streaking to identify the female Red-winged.

Stan's Notes: One of the most widespread and numerous birds in Texas. Found around marshes, wetlands, lakes and rivers. Flocks with as many as 10,000 birds have been reported. Males arrive before females and sing to defend their territory. The male repeats his call from the top of a cattail while showing off his red-and-yellow shoulder patches. The female chooses a mate and often builds her nest over shallow water in a thick stand of cattails. The male can be aggressive when defending the nest. Feeds mostly on seeds in spring and fall, and insects throughout the summer.

male
p. 29

female

Eastern
Towhee

Spotted Towhee
Pipilo maculatus

YEAR-ROUND
WINTER

Size: 8½" (22 cm)

Female: Brown head, dirty red-brown sides and a white belly. Multiple white spots on wings and sides. Long black tail with a white tip. Rich, red eyes.

Male: mostly black, lacking the brown head

Juvenile: brown with a heavily streaked chest

Nest: cup; female builds; 1–2 broods per year

Eggs: 3–5; white with brown markings

Incubation: 12–14 days; female and male incubate

Fledging: 10–12 days; female and male feed young

Migration: partial migrator to non-migrator

Food: seeds, fruit, insects

Compare: American Robin (p. 315) is larger.

Stan's Notes: The Spotted Towhee and Eastern Towhee were once considered a single species called Rufous-sided Towhee. Found in a variety of habitats, from thick brush and chaparral to suburban backyards. Usually heard noisily scratching through dead leaves on the ground for food. Over 70 percent of its diet is plant material. Eats more insects during spring and summer. Well known to retreat from danger by walking away rather than taking to flight. Nest is nearly always on the ground under bushes but away from where the male perches to sing. Begins breeding in April. Lays eggs in May. After the breeding season, moves to higher elevations. Song and plumage vary geographically and aren't well studied or understood.

female

male

Common Nighthawk

Chordeiles minor

SUMMER

Size: 9" (23 cm)

Male: Camouflaged brown and white with a white chin. Distinctive white band across the wings and tail, seen only in flight.

Female: similar to male, with a tan chin; lacks a white tail band

Juvenile: similar to female

Nest: no nest; lays eggs on the ground, usually on rocks, or on rooftop; 1 brood per year

Eggs: 2; cream with lavender markings

Incubation: 19–20 days; female and male incubate

Fledging: 20–21 days; female and male feed the young

Migration: complete, to South America

Food: insects caught in the air

Compare: The Chimney Swift (p. 131) is much smaller. Look for the white chin, obvious white band on the wings and characteristic flap-flap-flap-glide pattern to help identify the Common Nighthawk.

Stan's Notes: Usually only seen in flight at dusk or after sunset but not uncommon to see it sleeping on a branch during the day. A prolific insect eater and very noisy in flight, repeating a "peenting" call. Alternates slow wingbeats with bursts of quick wingbeats. In cities, prefers to nest on flat rooftops with gravel. City populations are on the decline as gravel rooftops are converted to other styles. In spring, the male performs a showy mating ritual consisting of a steep diving flight ending with a loud popping noise. One of the first birds to migrate in fall, starting in August. A summer resident throughout Texas. Often seen in large flocks.

Burrowing Owl
Athene cunicularia

YEAR-ROUND
SUMMER

Size: 9–10" (24 cm); up to 2' wingspan

Male: Brown owl with bold white spots and a white belly. Yellow eyes. Very long legs.

Female: same as male

Juvenile: same as adult, but belly is brown

Nest: cavity, former underground mammal den; female and male line den; 1 brood per year

Eggs: 6–11; white without markings

Incubation: 26–30 days; female incubates

Fledging: 25–28 days; female and male feed young

Migration: non-migrator to partial migrator in Texas

Food: insects, mammals, lizards, birds

Compare: Eastern Screech-Owl (p. 307) is slightly smaller and has ear tufts. Great Horned Owl (p. 261) is more than twice the size of Burrowing and has feather tuft "horns." Burrowing spends most of its time on the ground, unlike tree-loving Great Horned.

Stan's Notes: An owl of fields, open backyards, golf courses and airports. Nests in large family units or in small colonies. Takes over the underground dens of mammals, occasionally widening its den by kicking dirt backward. Lines den with cow pies, horse dung, grass and feathers. Some people have had success attracting these owls to their backyards by creating artificial dens. Often seen during the day, standing or sleeping around den entrance. Male brings food to incubating female, often moving family to a new den when young are just a few weeks old. Will bob head up and down while doing deep knee bends when agitated or threatened.

in flight

juvenile

male

female

in-flight juvenile

American Kestrel
Falco sparverius

YEAR-ROUND

Size: 9–11" (23–28 cm); up to 2' wingspan

Male: Rust-brown back and tail. White breast with dark spots. Two vertical black lines on a white face. Blue-gray wings. Wide black band with a white edge on the tip of a rusty tail.

Female: similar to male but slightly larger, with rust-brown wings and dark bands on the tail

Juvenile: same as adult of the same sex

Nest: cavity; does not build a nest; 1 brood per year

Eggs: 4–5; white with brown markings

Incubation: 29–31 days; male and female incubate

Fledging: 30–31 days; female and male feed the young

Migration: non-migrator to partial migrator in Texas

Food: insects, small mammals and birds, reptiles

Compare: The Peregrine Falcon (p. 337) is much larger and has a dark "hood" marking. No other small bird of prey has a rusty back and tail.

Stan's Notes: An unusual raptor because the sexes look different (dimorphic). Due to its small size, this falcon was once called a Sparrow Hawk. Hovers near roads, then dives for prey. Watch for it to pump its tail after landing on a perch. Perches nearly upright. Eats many grasshoppers. Adapts quickly to a wooden nest box. Can be extremely vocal, giving a loud series of high-pitched calls. Ability to see ultraviolet (UV) light helps it locate mice and other prey by their urine, which glows bright yellow in UV light.

male
p. 33

female

Yellow-headed Blackbird

Xanthocephalus xanthocephalus

MIGRATION
WINTER

Size:	9–11" (23–28 cm)
Female:	Large brown bird with a dull-yellow head and chest. Slightly smaller than the male.
Male:	black bird with a lemon-yellow head, breast and nape of neck, black mask, gray bill and white wing patches
Juvenile:	similar to female
Nest:	cup; female builds; 2 broods per year
Eggs:	3–5; greenish white with brown markings
Incubation:	11–13 days; female incubates
Fledging:	9–12 days; female feeds the young
Migration:	complete, to western parts of Texas, Mexico
Food:	insects, seeds; will come to ground feeders
Compare:	Female Red-winged Blackbird (p. 181) is smaller and has white eyebrows and heavy streaking. Look for the dull-yellow head to help identify the female Yellow-headed.

Stan's Notes: Found around marshes, wetlands and lakes. Nests in deep water, unlike its cousin, the Red-winged Blackbird, which prefers shallow water. Usually heard before seen. Gives a raspy, low, metallic-sounding call. The male is the only large black bird with a bright-yellow head. He gives an impressive mating display, flying with his head drooped and feet and tail pointing down while steadily beating his wings. Young keep low and out of sight for up to three weeks before they start to fly. Migrates in large flocks of as many as 200 birds, often with Red-winged Blackbirds and Brown-headed Cowbirds. Flocks of mainly males return in early April; females return later. Most colonies consist of 20–100 nests.

Killdeer
Charadrius vociferus

YEAR-ROUND

Size: 11" (28 cm)

Male: Upland shorebird with 2 black bands around the neck, like a necklace. Brown back and white belly. Bright reddish-orange rump, visible in flight.

Female: same as male

Juvenile: similar to adults, with a single neck band

Nest: ground; male scrapes; 2 broods per year

Eggs: 3–5; tan with brown markings

Incubation: 24–28 days; male and female incubate

Fledging: 25 days; male and female lead their young to food

Migration: non-migrator in Texas

Food: insects, worms, snails

Compare: The Spotted Sandpiper (p. 173) is found around water and lacks the 2 neck bands of the Killdeer.

Stan's Notes: Technically classified as a shorebird but lives in dry habitats instead of the shore. Often found in vacant fields, gravel pits, driveways, wetland edges or along railroad tracks. The only shorebird that has two black neck bands. Known to fake a broken wing to draw intruders away from the nest; once the nest is safe, the parent will take flight. Nests are just a slight depression in a dry area and are often hard to see. Hatchlings look like miniature adults walking on stilts. Soon after hatching, the young follow their parents around and peck for insects. Gives a loud and distinctive "kill-deer" call. Migrates in small flocks.

Brown Thrasher
Toxostoma rufum

YEAR-ROUND
SUMMER
WINTER

Size: 11" (28 cm)

Male: Rust-red with a long tail. Heavy streaking on the breast and belly. Two white wing bars. Long, curved bill and bright-yellow eyes.

Female: same as male

Juvenile: same as adults but with grayish eyes

Nest: cup; female and male build; 2 broods per year

Eggs: 4–5; pale blue with brown markings

Incubation: 11–14 days; female and male incubate

Fledging: 10–13 days; female and male feed the young

Migration: complete to non-migrator in Texas

Food: insects, fruit

Compare: The Curve-billed Thrasher (p. 319) is similar in size, but it has a longer bill with more curvature and lacks the rusty red color. American Robin (p. 315) and Gray Catbird (p. 309) are similar but smaller and lack a streaked chest, rusty color and yellow eyes. Look for the long rusty-red tail to help identify the Brown Thrasher.

Stan's Notes: A prodigious songster. Sings along forest edges and in suburban yards. Often found in thick shrubs, where it will sing deliberate musical phrases, repeating each twice. The male Brown Thrasher has the largest documented repertoire of all North American songbirds, with more than 1,100 types of songs. Builds nest low in dense shrubs, often in fencerows. Quickly flies or runs on the ground in and out of thick shrubs. A noisy feeder due to its habit of turning over leaves, small rocks and branches to find food.

male

yellow-shafted female

red-shafted male

red-shafted female

Northern Flicker
Colaptes auratus

Size: 12" (30 cm)

Male: Brown and black with a black mustache and black necklace. Red spot on the nape of the neck. Speckled chest. Large white rump patch, seen only when flying.

Female: same as male but without a black mustache

Juvenile: same as adult of the same sex

Nest: cavity; female and male excavate; 1 brood per year

Eggs: 5–8; white without markings

Incubation: 11–14 days; female and male incubate

Fledging: 25–28 days; female and male feed the young

Migration: non-migrator to partial migrator in Texas

Food: insects (especially ants and beetles); comes to suet feeders

Compare: The male Yellow-bellied Sapsucker (p. 67) has a red chin. The male Red-bellied Woodpecker (p. 73) has a red crown. Flickers are the only brown-backed woodpeckers in Texas.

Stan's Notes: This is the only woodpecker to regularly feed on the ground. Prefers ants and beetles and produces an antacid saliva that neutralizes the acidic defense of ants. Can be attracted to your yard with a nest box stuffed with sawdust. Yellow-shafted variety has golden-yellow wing linings and tails. Male yellow-shafteds have black mustaches; male red-shafteds have red mustaches. Hybrids between varieties occur in the Great Plains, where ranges overlap. Often reuses an old nest. Undulates deeply during flight, flashing yellow under its wings and tail and calling "wacka-wacka" loudly. Populations swell in winter with northern migrants.

Mourning Dove
Zenaida macroura

YEAR-ROUND

Size: 12" (30 cm)

Male: Smooth and fawn-colored. Gray patch on the head. Iridescent pink and greenish blue on the neck. Black spot behind and below the eyes. Black spots on the wings and tail. Pointed, wedged tail; white edges seen in flight.

Female: similar to male, but lacks the pink-and-green iridescent neck feathers

Juvenile: spotted and streaked plumage

Nest: platform; female and male build; 2 broods per year

Eggs: 2; white without markings

Incubation: 13–14 days; male incubates during the day, female incubates at night

Fledging: 12–14 days; female and male feed the young

Migration: non-migrator to partial migrator; will move around to find food

Food: seeds; will visit seed and ground feeders

Compare: Eurasian Collared-Dove (p. 329) has a black collar on the nape of its neck. White-winged Dove (p. 321) is similar, but it has a white edge on its wings.

Stan's Notes: Name comes from its mournful cooing. A ground feeder, bobbing its head as it walks. One of the few birds to drink without lifting its head, like the Rock Pigeon (p. 331). The parents feed the young (squab) a regurgitated liquid called crop-milk for their first few days of life. Platform nest is flimsy and often falls apart in storms. During takeoff and in flight, wind rushes through the bird's wing feathers, creating a characteristic whistling sound.

winter

breeding

Pied-billed Grebe
Podilymbus podiceps

YEAR-ROUND

Size: 12–14" (30–36 cm)

Male: Small and brown with a black chin and fluffy white patch beneath the tail. Black ring around a thick, chicken-like, ivory bill. Winter bill is brown and unmarked.

Female: same as male

Juvenile: paler than adults, with white spots and a gray chest, belly and bill

Nest: floating platform; female and male build; 1 brood per year

Eggs: 5–7; bluish white without markings

Incubation: 22–24 days; female and male incubate

Fledging: 45–60 days; female and male feed the young

Migration: complete to non-migrator in Texas

Food: crayfish, aquatic insects, fish

Compare: Look for a puffy white patch under the tail and thick, chicken-like bill to help identify.

Stan's Notes: A common resident water bird, often seen diving for food. When disturbed, it slowly sinks like a submarine, quickly compressing its feathers, forcing the air out. Was called Hell-diver due to the length of time it can stay submerged. Able to surface far from where it went under. Well suited to life on water, with short wings, lobed toes, and legs set close to the rear of its body. Swims easily but moves awkwardly on land. Very sensitive to pollution. Builds nest on a floating mat in water. "Grebe" may originate from the Breton word *krib*, meaning "crest," referring to the crested head plumes of many grebes, especially during breeding season.

male
p. 83

female

Bufflehead
Bucephala albeola

WINTER

Size: 13–15" (33–38 cm)

Female: Brownish-gray duck with a dark-brown head. White patch on cheek, just behind the eyes.

Male: striking black-and-white duck with a large bonnet-like white patch on the back of head; head shines greenish purple in sunlight

Juvenile: similar to female

Nest: cavity; female lines an old woodpecker cavity; 1 brood per year

Eggs: 8–10; ivory-to-olive without markings

Incubation: 29–31 days; female incubates

Fledging: 50–55 days; female leads the young to food

Migration: complete, to Texas, Mexico, Central America

Food: aquatic insects, crustaceans, mollusks

Compare: Lesser Scaup (p. 225) is slightly larger and has a white patch at the base of the bill. Look for the white cheek patch to help identify the female Bufflehead.

Stan's Notes: A small, common diving duck, almost always seen in small groups or with other duck species on rivers, ponds and lakes. Nests in vacant woodpecker holes. When cavities in trees are scarce, known to use a burrow in an earthen bank or will use a nest box. Lines the cavity with fluffy down feathers. Unlike other ducks, the young stay in the nest for up to two days before they venture out with their mothers. The female is very territorial and remains with the same mate for many years.

Greater Yellowlegs
Tringa melanoleuca

MIGRATION
WINTER

Size:	13–15" (33–38 cm)
Male:	Tall with a bulbous head and a long, thin, slightly upturned bill. Gray streaking on the chest. White belly. Long yellow legs.
Female:	same as male
Juvenile:	same as adults
Nest:	ground; female builds; 1 brood per year
Eggs:	3–4; off-white with brown markings
Incubation:	22–23 days; female and male incubate
Fledging:	18–20 days; male and female feed the young
Migration:	complete, to Texas, Mexico, Central America and South America
Food:	small fish, aquatic insects
Compare:	Breeding Willet (p. 211) is slightly larger, with a shorter neck and larger head, and it lacks bright-yellow legs. The breeding Spotted Sandpiper (p. 173) has spots on its chest. Look for the long yellow legs and long bill to identify the Greater Yellowlegs.

Stan's Notes: A common shorebird that can be identified by the slightly upturned bill and long yellow legs, which enable it to wade in deep water. Often seen resting on one leg. Rushes forward through the water to feed, plowing its bill or swinging it from side to side, catching small fish and insects. A skittish bird, it is quick to give an alarm call, causing flocks to take flight. Typically moves into the water before taking flight. Gives a variety of "flight" notes at takeoff. Nests on the ground close to water on the northern tundra of Labrador and Newfoundland.

male
p. 41

female

Boat-tailed Grackle
Quiscalus major

YEAR-ROUND

Size: 13–15" (33–38 cm), female
15–17" (38–43 cm), male

Female: A golden-brown chest and head. Nearly black wings and tail. Female is non-iridescent.

Male: iridescent blue-black bird with a very long tail and dark eyes

Juvenile: similar to female

Nest: cup; female builds; 2 broods per year

Eggs: 2–4; pale greenish blue with brown marks

Incubation: 13–15 days; female incubates

Fledging: 12–15 days; female feeds the young

Migration: non-migrator; moves around to find food

Food: insects, berries, seeds, fish; visits feeders

Compare: Fairly distinctive. Not confused with many other birds. Found only along the coast.

Stan's Notes: A noisy bird of coastal saltwater and inland marshes, giving several harsh, high-pitched calls and several squeaks. Eats a wide variety of foods from grains to fish. Sometimes seen picking insects off the backs of cattle. Will also visit bird feeders. Makes a cup nest with mud or cow dung and grass. Nests in small colonies. Most nesting occurs in April and May. Boat-taileds in Texas and on the Gulf Coast have dark eyes. Birds further east, on the Atlantic Coast, have bright-red eyes.

male
p. 43

female

Great-tailed Grackle

Quiscalus mexicanus

YEAR-ROUND

Size: 15" (38 cm), female
18" (45 cm), male

Female: An overall brown bird with a gray-to-brown belly. Light-brown-to-white eyes, eyebrows, throat and upper portion of chest.

Male: all-black bird with iridescent purple sheen on head and back, exceptionally long tail, bright-yellow eyes

Juvenile: similar to female

Nest: cup; female builds; 1–2 broods per year

Eggs: 3–5; greenish blue with brown markings

Incubation: 12–14 days; female incubates

Fledging: 21–23 days; female feeds young

Migration: non-migrator to partial in Texas; moves around to find food

Food: insects, fruit, seeds; comes to seed feeders

Compare: The female Boat-tailed Grackle (p. 207) is similar but it is found along the coast. The Great-tailed female is much larger than the female Brown-headed Cowbird (p. 165).

Stan's Notes: This is our largest grackle. It was once considered a subspecies of the Boat-tailed Grackle, which occurs along the Gulf Coast. Prefers to nest close to water in an open habitat. A colony nester. Males do not participate in nest building, incubation or raising young. Males rarely fight; females squabble over nest sites and materials. Several females mate with one male. The species is expanding northward, moving into northern states. Western populations tend to be larger than eastern. Song varies from population to population.

breeding

winter
p. 333

displaying

Willet
Catoptrophorus semipalmatus

YEAR-ROUND
MIGRATION

Size: 14–16" (36–40 cm)

Male: Brown breeding plumage with a white belly. Brown bill and legs. Distinctive black-and-white wing lining pattern, seen in flight or during display.

Female: same as male

Juvenile: similar to breeding adult, more tan in color

Nest: ground; female builds; 1 brood per year

Eggs: 3–5; olive-green with dark markings

Incubation: 24–28 days; male and female incubate

Fledging: 1–2 days; female and male feed young

Migration: complete, to coastal Texas, Mexico, Central America and South America; year-round resident on the Gulf Coast

Food: insects, small fish, crabs, worms, clams

Compare: Greater Yellowlegs (p. 205) is slightly smaller and has a smaller head, longer neck and yellow legs. Look for Willet's distinctive black-and-white wing linings.

Stan's Notes: Seen during migration throughout Texas and a year-round resident along the coast. Northern birds pass through coastal Texas to destinations farther south. It appears a rich, warm brown during the breeding season and rather plain gray during the winter, but it always has a striking black-and-white wing pattern when seen in flight. Uses its black-and-white wing patches to display to its mate. Named after the "pill-will-willet" call it gives during the breeding season. Gives a "kip-kip-kip" alarm call when it takes flight. Nests along the Gulf and East Coasts, in some western states and Canada.

Green-winged Teal
Anas crecca

WINTER

Size: 14–15" (36–38 cm)

Male: Chestnut head with a dark-green patch outlined with white from the eyes to the nape of neck. Gray body and butter-yellow tail. Green patch on the wings (speculum), seen in flight.

Female: light-brown duck with black spots and a green speculum, small bill

Juvenile: same as female

Nest: ground; female builds; 1 brood per year

Eggs: 8–10; cream-white without markings

Incubation: 21–23 days; female incubates

Fledging: 32–34 days; female teaches the young to feed

Migration: complete, to Texas

Food: aquatic plants and insects

Compare: Male Wood Duck (p. 363) is more colorful than male Green-winged. Female Cinnamon Teal (p. 219) is similar to female Green-winged, but it has a dark line through the eyes and a larger bill. Female Blue-winged Teal (p. 217) is similar in size, but it is slightly white at the base of its bill.

Stan's Notes: One of the smallest dabbling ducks. Tips forward in water to feed off the bottom of shallow ponds. This behavior makes it vulnerable to ingesting spent lead shot, which can cause death. It walks well on land and will also feed in flooded fields and woodlands. Known for its fast and agile flight. Groups wheel and spin through the air in tight formation. The green wing patches are most obvious during flight.

winter male

male

female

Ruddy Duck
Oxyura jamaicensis

WINTER

Size: 15" (38 cm)

Male: Compact reddish-brown body. Black crown and nape. Large bright-white cheek patch. Distinctive light-blue bill. Long tail, often raised above water. Winter has a dull brown-to-gray body and dark bill.

Female: similar to winter male, lacks the large white cheek patch and blue bill

Juvenile: similar to female

Nest: ground; female builds; 1 brood per year

Eggs: 6–8; pale white without markings

Incubation: 23–26 days; female incubates

Fledging: 42–48 days; female and male feed young

Migration: complete, to Texas

Food: aquatic insects and plants

Compare: The male Ring-necked Duck (p. 89) has gray sides and a white ring around the bill. Look for the light-blue bill and raised tail of the male Ruddy Duck.

Stan's Notes: A diving duck with a unique appearance. Awkward on land. Often secretive, found on ponds and bays. Flushes quickly and stays away for a long time. Breeding male displays like a windup toy, ratcheting his head up and down, making muffled sounds and a staccato "pop." Male breeds with more than one female. Female lays some eggs in other duck nests. Male often seen with female and ducklings, but is not the father. Babies can dive soon after hatching. Has a blue bill, but is not the species that duck hunters call Blue Bill.

Blue-winged Teal
Spatula discors

YEAR-ROUND
SUMMER
MIGRATION
WINTER

Size: 15–16" (38–41 cm)

Male: Small, plain-looking brown duck with black speckles and a large, crescent-shaped white mark at the base of the bill. Gray head. Black tail with a small white patch. Blue wing patch (speculum), best seen in flight.

Female: duller than male, with only slight white at the base of the bill; lacks a crescent mark on the face and a white patch on the tail

Juvenile: same as female

Nest: ground; female builds; 1 brood per year

Eggs: 8–11; creamy white

Incubation: 23–27 days; female incubates

Fledging: 35–44 days; female feeds the young

Migration: complete, to Texas, Mexico and Central America; non-migrator in parts of Texas

Food: aquatic plants, seeds, aquatic insects

Compare: The female Mallard (p. 243) has an orange-and-black bill. The female Wood Duck (p. 233) has a crest. Female Green-winged Teal (p. 213) is similar in size but lacks white at base of bill. Look for the white facial mark to identify the male Blue-winged.

Stan's Notes: One of the smallest ducks in North America and one of the longest-distance migrating ducks, with widespread nesting as far north as Alaska. Constructs nest some distance from water. Female performs a distraction display to protect nest and young. Male leaves female near the end of incubation. Planting crops and cultivating to pond edges have caused a decline in population.

male

female

Cinnamon Teal
Anas cyanoptera

SUMMER
MIGRATION
WINTER

Size: 16" (40 cm)

Male: Deep cinnamon head, neck and belly. Light brown back. Dark-gray bill. Deep-red eyes. Non-breeding male is overall brown with a red tinge.

Female: overall brown with a pale-brown head, long shovel-like bill, green patch on wings

Juvenile: similar to female

Nest: ground; female builds; 1 brood per year

Eggs: 7–12; pinkish white without markings

Incubation: 21–25 days; female incubates

Fledging: 40–50 days; female teaches young to feed

Migration: parital migrator to complete, to southern Texas, Mexico

Food: aquatic plants and insects, seeds

Compare: Northern Shoveler (p. 241) also has cinnamon sides, but it is larger and has a green head and very large spoon-shaped bill. Female Green-winged Teal (p. 213) is similar to the Female Cinnamon Teal, but the Green-winged is smaller and has a dark line through its eyes.

Stan's Notes: The male is one of the most stunningly beautiful ducks. When threatened, the female feigns a wing injury to lure the predator away from her young. Prefers to nest along alkaline marshes and shallow lakes, within 75 yards (68 m) of the water. Mallards and other ducks often lay eggs in teal nests, resulting in many nests with over 15 eggs.

soaring

Red-shouldered Hawk
Buteo lineatus

YEAR-ROUND

Size: 15–19" (38–48 cm); up to 3½' wingspan

Male: Reddish (cinnamon) head, shoulders, breast and belly. Wings and back are dark brown with white spots. Long tail with thin white bands and wide black bands. Obvious red wing linings, seen in flight.

Female: same as male

Juvenile: similar to adults but lacks the cinnamon color; white chest with dark spots

Nest: platform; female and male build; 1 brood per year

Eggs: 2–4; white with dark markings

Incubation: 27–29 days; female and male incubate

Fledging: 39–45 days; female and male feed the young

Migration: non-migrator in Texas

Food: reptiles, amphibians, large insects, birds

Compare: The Red-tailed Hawk (p. 253) has a white chest. Cooper's Hawk (p. 335) has a slimmer body and longer tail. The Sharp-shinned Hawk (p. 325) is smaller and lacks the reddish head and belly of the Red-shouldered Hawk.

Stan's Notes: A woodland hawk, seen in backyards. Likes to hunt at forest edges, spotting snakes, frogs, insects, occasional small birds and other prey as it perches. Often flaps with an alternating gliding pattern. Very vocal with a distinct scream. Breeds when it reaches 2–3 years. Remains in the same territory for many years. Starts constructing its nest in February. Young leave the nest by June.

Barn Owl
Tyto alba

YEAR-ROUND

Size: 16–19" (40–48 cm); up to 4' wingspan

Male: "Non-eared" owl with a rusty-brown back of head, back, wings and tail. Heart-shaped white face, outlined in darker rusty brown. White chest and belly. Dark eyes. Long gray legs. Gray feet. Yellow bill.

Female: similar to male, often with a rusty wash over the chest and belly

Juvenile: light gray to white; fuzzy-looking overall

Nest: cavity, occasionally on a cliff crevice; female builds; 1 brood per year

Eggs: 3–7; white without markings

Incubation: 30–34 days; female incubates

Fledging: 52–56 days; male and female feed the young

Migration: non-migrator

Food: small mammals, birds, snakes

Compare: Burrowing Owl (p. 187) is smaller and lacks the heart-shaped white face of the Barn Owl. The Eastern Screech-Owl (p. 307) is smaller, has ear tufts and lacks the white face of the Barn Owl.

Stan's Notes: This owl is well known for nesting in old barns (hence the common name) but will also nest in any dark cavity, on cliffs or in trees. The male feeds the female during incubation. Clutch size depends on the availability of prey: the more prey, the larger the clutch. Young hatch one per day (asynchronously) over two weeks, creating a range of ages in the nest. Will sway back and forth with lowered head when confronted.

male p. 85

female

Lesser Scaup
Aythya affinis

WINTER

Size: 16–17" (40–43 cm)

Female: Overall brown duck with a dull-white patch at the base of a light-gray bill. Yellow eyes.

Male: white and gray; the chest and head appear nearly black but the head looks purple with green highlights in direct sun; yellow eyes

Juvenile: same as female

Nest: ground; female builds; 1 brood per year

Eggs: 8–14; olive-buff without markings

Incubation: 22–28 days; female incubates

Fledging: 45–50 days; female teaches young to feed

Migration: complete, to Texas, Mexico, Central America and northern South America

Food: aquatic plants and insects

Compare: Compare: Female Ring-necked Duck (p. 229) is a similar size but has a white ring around the bill. Male Blue-winged Teal (p. 217) is slightly smaller and has a crescent-shaped white mark at the base of bill. Female Wood Duck (p. 233) is larger with white around eyes.

Stan's Notes: A common diving duck. Often seen in large flocks on lakes, ponds and sewage lagoons. Submerges itself completely to feed on the bottom of lakes (unlike dabbling ducks, which only tip forward to reach the bottom). Note the bold white stripe under the wings when in flight. The male leaves the female when she starts incubating eggs. The quantity of eggs (clutch size) increases with the female's age. This species has an interesting babysitting arrangement in which groups of young (crèches) are tended by one to three adult females. A winter resident throughout Texas.

male
p. 87

female

Hooded Merganser
Lophodytes cucullatus

WINTER

Size: 16–19" (41–48 cm)

Female: Sleek brown-and-rust bird with a red head. Ragged "hair" on the back of the head. Long, thin, brown bill.

Male: black back, rust-brown sides, long black bill; raises crest "hood" to display a white patch

Juvenile: similar to female

Nest: cavity; female lines an old woodpecker cavity or a nest box near water; 1 brood per year

Eggs: 10–12; white without markings

Incubation: 32–33 days; female incubates

Fledging: 71 days; female feeds the young

Migration: complete, to the eastern half of Texas

Food: small fish, aquatic insects, crustaceans (especially crayfish)

Compare: Female Lesser Scaup (p. 225) is smaller and has a dull-white patch at the base of its bill. Look for the ragged "hair" on the back of the head of the female Hoodie.

Stan's Notes: A small diving duck, found in shallow ponds, sloughs, lakes and rivers. Usually in small groups. Quick, low flight across the water, with fast wingbeats. Male has a deep, rolling call. Female gives a hoarse quack. Nests in wooded areas. Female will lay some eggs in the nests of other mergansers, goldeneyes or Wood Ducks (egg dumping), resulting in 20–25 eggs in some nests. Rarely, she shares a nest, sitting with a Wood Duck.

male p. 89

female

Ring-necked Duck
Aythya collaris

WINTER

Size: 16–19" (41–48 cm)

Female: Brown with a darker brown back and crown and lighter-brown sides. Gray face. White eye-ring with a white line behind the eye. White ring around the bill. Peaked head.

Male: black head, chest and back; gray-to-white sides; blue bill with a bold white ring and a thinner ring at the base; peaked head

Juvenile: similar to female

Nest: ground; female builds; 1 brood per year

Eggs: 8–10; olive to brown without markings

Incubation: 26–27 days; female incubates

Fledging: 49–56 days; female teaches the young to feed

Migration: complete, to Texas, Mexico, Central America

Food: aquatic plants and insects

Compare: Female Lesser Scaup (p. 225) is similar in size. Look for the white ring around the bill to help identify the female Ring-necked Duck.

Stan's Notes: A common winter duck throughout Texas. Often seen in larger freshwater lakes, usually in small flocks or just pairs. A diving duck, watch for it to dive underwater to forage for food. Springs up off the water to take flight. Has a distinctive tall, peaked head with a sloped forehead. Flattens its crown when diving. Male gives a quick series of grating barks and grunts. Female gives high-pitched peeps. Named "Ring-necked" for its cinnamon collar, which is nearly impossible to see in the field. Also called Ring-billed Duck due to the white ring on its bill.

Whimbrel
Numenius phaeopus

WINTER

Size: 18" (45 cm)

Male: Heavily streaked bird, light brown to gray. A long down-curved bill and multiple dark brown stripes on crown. Dark line through eyes. Legs are light gray to blue.

Female: same as male

Juvenile: similar to adult

Nest: ground; female and male construct; 1 brood per year

Eggs: 3–4; olive-green with dark markings

Incubation: 27–28 days; male and female incubate

Fledging: 35–42 days; female and male feed the young

Migration: complete, to coastal Texas, Mexico, Central America and South America

Food: insects, snails, worms, leeches, berries

Compare: The breeding Willet (p. 211) is smaller, lacks a crown with brown stripes and long, down-curved bill. Greater Yellowlegs (p. 205) is smaller and has yellow legs.

Stan's Notes: A winter resident, easily identified by its very long down-curved bill and brown stripes on head. Uses its bill to probe deep into sand and mud for insects. Unlike the other shorebirds, berries become an important food source in summer. Is very vocal, giving single note whistles. Returns to tundra of northern Alaska to nest. Doesn't breed until age 3. Has a long-term pair bond. Adults leave breeding grounds up to two weeks before the young leave.

male
p. 363

female

Wood Duck
Aix sponsa

Size: 17–20" (43–51 cm)

Female: Small brown dabbling duck. Bright-white eye-ring and a not-so-obvious crest. Blue patch on wings (speculum), often hidden.

Male: highly ornamented, with a mostly green head and crest patterned with black and white; rusty chest, white belly and red eyes

Juvenile: similar to female

Nest: cavity; female lines an old woodpecker cavity or a nest box in a tree; 1 brood per year

Eggs: 10–15; creamy white without markings

Incubation: 28–36 days; female incubates

Fledging: 56–68 days; female teaches the young to feed

Migration: non-migrator to partial migrator in Texas

Food: aquatic insects, plants, seeds

Compare: The female Mallard (p. 243) and female Blue-winged Teal (p. 217) lack the eye-ring and crest. The female Northern Shoveler (p. 241) is larger and has a large spoon-shaped bill.

Stan's Notes: A common duck of quiet, shallow backwater ponds. Nearly went extinct around 1900 due to overhunting, but it's doing well now. Nests in a tree cavity or a nest box in a tree. Seen flying in forests or perching on high branches. Female takes off with a loud, squealing call and enters the nest cavity from full flight. Lays some eggs in a neighboring nest (egg dumping), resulting in more than 20 eggs in some clutches. Hatchlings stay in the nest for 24 hours, then jump from as high as 60 feet (18 m) to the ground or water to follow their mother. They never return to the nest.

male

female

WINTER

American Wigeon
Mareca americana

Size: 18–20" (48 cm)

Male: Brown duck with a rounded head and obvious white cap. Deep-green patch starting behind the eyes and streaking down the neck. Long pointed tail. Short, black-tipped grayish bill. White belly and wing linings, seen in flight. Non-breeding lacks white cap and green patch.

Female: light brown with a pale gray head, a short, black-tipped grayish bill, green wing patch (speculum) and dark eye spot; white belly and wing linings, seen in flight

Juvenile: similar to female

Nest: ground; female builds; 1 brood per year

Eggs: 7–12; white without markings

Incubation: 23–25 days; female incubates

Fledging: 37–48 days; female teaches the young to feed

Migration: complete, to Texas, other southern states

Food: aquatic plants, seeds

Compare: Male American Wigeon is easily identified by the white cap and black-tipped grayish bill. Look for the black-tipped grayish bill and green wing patch to help identify the female American Wigeon.

Stan's Notes: Often in small flocks or with other ducks. Prefers shallow lakes. Male stays with the female only during the first week of incubation. Female raises the young. If threatened, female feigns injury while the young run and hide. Conceals upland nest in tall vegetation within 50–250 yards (46–229 m) of water.

male
p. 341

female

Gadwall
Mareca strepera

YEAR-ROUND
WINTER

Size: 19" (48 cm)

Female: Mottled brown with a pronounced color change from dark-brown body to light-brown neck and head. Bright-white wing linings, seen in flight. Small white wing patch, seen when swimming. Gray bill with orange sides.

Male: plump gray duck with a brown head and distinctive black rump, white belly, bright-white wing linings, small white wing patch, chestnut-tinged wings, gray bill

Juvenile: similar to female

Nest: ground; female lines the nest with fine grass and down feathers plucked from her chest; 1 brood per year

Eggs: 8–11; white without markings

Incubation: 24–27 days; female incubates

Fledging: 48–56 days; young feed themselves

Migration: complete to non-migrator in Texas

Food: aquatic insects

Compare: Female Mallard (p. 243) is similar but has a blue-and-white wing mark. Look for Gadwall's white wing patch and gray bill with orange sides.

Stan's Notes: A duck of shallow marshes. Consumes mostly plant material, dunking its head in water to feed rather than tipping forward, like other dabbling ducks. Walks well on land; feeds in fields and woodlands. Nests within 300 feet (90 m) of water. Often in pairs with other duck species. Establishes pair bond during winter.

male p. 387

female

Redhead
Aythya americana

WINTER

Size: 19" (48 cm)

Female: Soft-brown, plain-looking duck with gray to white wing linings. Rounded top of head. Two-toned bill, gray with a black tip.

Male: rich-red head and neck with a black chest and tail, gray sides, smoky-gray wings and back, tricolored bill with a light-blue base, white ring and black tip

Juvenile: similar to female

Nest: cup; female builds; 1 brood per year

Eggs: 9–14; pale white without markings

Incubation: 24–28 days; female and male incubate

Fledging: 56–73 days; female shows young what to eat

Migration: complete, to Texas

Food: seeds, aquatic plants, insects

Compare: Female Northern Shoveler (p. 241) is similar, but it is lighter brown and has an exceptionally large, shovel-shaped bill.

Stan's Notes: A duck of permanent large bodies of water. Forages along the shoreline, feeding on seeds, aquatic plants and insects. Usually builds nest directly on the water's surface, using large mats of vegetation. Female lays up to 75 percent of its eggs in the nests of other Redheads and several other duck species. Nests primarily in the Prairie Pothole region of the northern Great Plains. Overall populations seem to be increasing at about 2–3 percent each year. Winters throughout Texas where it can find water.

male p. 367

female

Northern Shoveler

Anas clypeata

WINTER

Size: 19–21" (48–53 cm)

Female: A medium-sized brown duck speckled with black. Green patch on the wings (speculum). An extraordinarily large, spoon-shaped bill.

Male: iridescent green head, rusty sides, white chest and a large spoon-shaped bill

Juvenile: same as female

Nest: ground; female builds; 1 brood per year

Eggs: 9–12; olive without markings

Incubation: 22–25 days; female incubates

Fledging: 30–60 days; female leads the young to food

Migration: complete, to Texas, Mexico, Central America

Food: aquatic insects, plants

Compare: Female Mallard (p. 243) is similar but lacks the Shoveler's large bill. Female Redhead (p. 239) is overall lighter brown and has a dark gray bill with a black tip. Look for Shoveler's large spoon-shaped bill to help identify.

Stan's Notes: One of several species of shovelers. Called "Shoveler" due to the peculiar, shovel-like shape of its bill. Given the common name "Northern" because it is the only species of these ducks in North America. Seen in shallow wetlands, ponds and small lakes in flocks of 5–10 birds. Flocks fly in tight formation. Swims low in water, pointing its large bill toward the water as if it's too heavy to lift. Usually swims in tight circles while feeding. Feeds mainly by filtering tiny aquatic insects and plants from the surface of the water with its bill. Winters in Texas where it can find water.

male
p. 365

female

Mallard
Anas platyrhynchos

YEAR-ROUND
WINTER

Size: 19–21" (48–53 cm)

Female: Brown duck with a blue-and-white wing mark (speculum). Orange-and-black bill.

Male: large green head, white necklace, rust-brown or chestnut chest, combination of gray-and-white sides, yellow bill, orange legs and feet

Juvenile: same as female but with a yellow bill

Nest: ground; female builds; 1 brood per year

Eggs: 7–10; greenish to whitish, unmarked

Incubation: 26–30 days; female incubates

Fledging: 42–52 days; female leads the young to food

Migration: non-migrator in Texas, joined by birds from further north in winter

Food: seeds, plants, aquatic insects; will come to ground feeders offering corn

Compare: Female Gadwall (p. 237) has a gray bill with orange sides. Female Northern Pintail (p. 245) is similar to female Mallard, but it has a gray bill. Female Northern Shoveler (p. 241) has a spoon-shaped bill. Female Wood Duck (p. 233) has a white eye-ring.

Stan's Notes: A familiar dabbling duck of lakes and ponds. Also found in rivers, streams and some backyards. Tips forward to feed on vegetation on the bottom of shallow water. The name "Mallard" comes from the Latin word *masculus,* meaning "male," referring to the male's habit of taking no part in raising the young. Female and male have white underwings and white tails, but only the male has black central tail feathers that curl upward. The female gives a classic quack. Returns to its birthplace each year.

Northern Pintail

Anas acuta

YEAR-ROUND
WINTER

Size: 20" (52 cm), female
25" (63 cm), male

Male: A slender, elegant duck with a brown head, white neck and gray body. Gray bill. Extremely long and narrow black tail. Non-breeding has a pale brown head that lacks the clear demarcation between the brown head and white neck. Lacks long tail feathers.

Female: mottled brown body with a paler head and neck, long tail, gray bill

Juvenile: similar to female

Nest: ground; female builds; 1 brood per year

Eggs: 6–9; olive-green without markings

Incubation: 22–25 days; female incubates

Fledging: 36–50 days; female teaches young to feed

Migration: complete, to Texas and Mexico

Food: aquatic plants and insects, seeds

Compare: The male Northern Pintail has a distinctive brown head and white neck and unique long tail feathers. Female Mallard (p. 243) is similar to female Pintail, but Mallard has an orange bill with black spots.

Stan's Notes: A common dabbling duck of marshes in the winter. About 90 percent of its diet is aquatic plants, except when females feed heavily on aquatic insects prior to nesting, presumably to gain extra nutrients for egg production. Male holds tail upright from the water's surface. No other North American duck has such a long tail.

male
p. 389

female

WINTER

Canvasback
Aythya valisineria

Size: 20½" (52 cm)

Female: Brown head, neck and chest. Light-gray-to-brown sides. Long sloping forehead that transitions into a long dark bill.

Male: deep-red head and neck, sloping forehead, long black bill, gray-and-white sides and back, black chest and tail

Juvenile: similar to female

Nest: ground; female builds; 1 brood per year

Eggs: 7–9; pale white to gray without markings

Incubation: 24–29 days; female incubates

Fledging: 56–67 days; female leads young to food

Migration: complete, to Texas and Mexico

Food: aquatic insects, small clams

Compare: Female Lesser Scaup (p. 225) is smaller, has a white marking at the base of its bill and lacks the sloping forehead and long dark bill of the female Canvasback.

Stan's Notes: A large inland duck of freshwater lakes, rivers and ponds. Populations declined dramatically in the 1960–80s due to marsh drainage for agriculture. Females return to their birthplace (philopatric) while males disperse to new areas. Will mate during migration or on the breeding grounds. A courting male gives a soft cooing call when displaying and during aerial chases. Male leaves the female after incubation starts. Female takes a new mate every year. Female feeds very little during incubation and will lose up to 70 percent of fat reserves during that time.

in flight

Black-bellied Whistling-Duck

Dendrocygna autumnalis

YEAR-ROUND

Size: 20–22" (50–56 cm)

Male: Overall rusty red to brown with a gray face and upper neck. Black sides, belly and tail. Bold white stripe on wings. Large red-to-orange bill with a gray tip (nail). White eye-ring. Long pink legs and feet.

Female: same as male

Juvenile: dull-brown-to-gray body, gray bill, legs and feet; lacks adult's black sides, belly and tail

Nest: cavity; female lines old woodpecker nest cavity, sometimes nests on ground along lakeshore; 1 brood per year

Eggs: 12–14; creamy white

Incubation: 25–30 days; female and male incubate

Fledging: 53–63 days; male and female lead young to food

Migration: non-migrator, moves around to find food

Food: seeds, grains, aquatic insects, snails

Compare: Male Cinnamon Teal (p. 219) is a similar rusty red, but it is smaller and lacks black sides and a reddish orange bill.

Stan's Notes: Can be common in parks with ponds. Male and female form a strong long-term pair bond, and the male helps incubate eggs; both are unusual for ducks. Females are known to dump their eggs in other nests, resulting in some females with dozens of eggs. Not all get incubated. Babies all leave the nest within 24 hours of hatching. Black-bellied Whistling-Duck is one of two duck species in North America (Fulvous Whistling-Duck is the other) in which the male and female look alike (not sexually dimorphic).

male
p. 339

female

soaring

Northern Harrier

Circus hudsonius

WINTER

Size: 18–22" (45–56 cm); up to 4' wingspan

Female: Slender, low-flying hawk with a dark-brown back and brown streaking on the chest and belly. Large white rump patch. Thin black tail bands and black wing tips. Yellow eyes.

Male: silver-gray with a large white rump patch and white belly, black wing tips, yellow eyes, faint, thin bands across the tail

Juvenile: similar to female, with an orange breast

Nest: ground; female and male construct; 1 brood per year

Eggs: 4–8; bluish white without markings

Incubation: 31–32 days; female incubates

Fledging: 30–35 days; male and female feed the young

Migration: complete, to Texas, Mexico, Central America

Food: mice, snakes, insects, small birds

Compare: Slimmer than the Red-tailed Hawk (p. 253). Look for the characteristic low gliding and the black tail bands to identify the female Harrier.

Stan's Notes: One of the easiest of hawks to identify. Glides just above the ground, following the contours of the land while searching for prey. Holds its wings just above horizontal, tilting back and forth in the wind, similar to the Turkey Vulture. Formerly called Marsh Hawk due to its habit of hunting over marshes. Feeds and nests on the ground. Will also preen and rest on the ground. Unlike other hawks, mainly uses its hearing to find prey, followed by its sight. At any age, it has a distinctive owl-like face disk.

Western

soaring

Eastern

juvenile
soaring

soaring

juvenile

Red-tailed Hawk
Buteo jamaicensis

YEAR-ROUND

Size: 19–23" (48–58 cm); up to 4½' wingspan

Male: Variety of colorations, from chocolate brown to nearly all white. Often brown with a white breast and brown belly band. Rust-red tail. Underside of wing is white with a small dark patch on the leading edge near the shoulder.

Female: same as male but slightly larger

Juvenile: similar to adults, with a speckled breast and light eyes; lacks a red tail

Nest: platform; male and female build; 1 brood per year

Eggs: 2–3; white without markings or sometimes marked with brown

Incubation: 30–35 days; female and male incubate

Fledging: 45–46 days; male and female feed the young

Migration: non-migrator to partial migrator

Food: small and medium-sized animals, large birds, snakes, fish, insects, bats, carrion

Compare: Red-shouldered Hawk (p. 221) and Sharp-shinned Hawk (p. 325) are much smaller.

Stan's Notes: Common in open country and cities. Seen perching on fences, freeway lampposts and trees. Look for it circling above open fields and roadsides, searching for prey. Gives a high-pitched scream that trails off. Often builds a large stick nest in large trees along roads. Lines nest with finer material, like evergreen needles. Returns to the same nest site each year. The red tail develops in the second year and is best seen from above. Western variety has a brown chin, while Eastern has a white chin. Map reflects the combined range.

soaring

juvenile

Harris's Hawk

Parabuteo unicinctus

YEAR-ROUND

Size: 20–22" (50 cm); up to 4' wingspan

Male: Overall dark brown hawk with rusty brown shoulders, wing linings and legs. Yellow base of bill. Bright white rump. Black tail with a bright white tip. Rusty wing linings, seen in flight. Long yellow legs. Yellow feet.

Female: same as male, but slightly larger

Juvenile: overall lighter brown with white streaks on breast, brown tail

Nest: platform; female and male build; 1–2 broods per year

Eggs: 3–4; pale white with some brown markings

Incubation: 33–36 days; female and male incubate

Fledging: 43–49 days; female and male feed young

Migration: non-migrator

Food: small mammals, snakes, birds, large insects

Compare: Red-tailed Hawk (p. 253) has a white breast and lacks rusty markings on wings. Look for Harris's white rump and white-tipped black tail.

Stan's Notes: Usually in semiarid woodlands near water. Common in city parks and suburban yards. Unlike most raptors, it hunts in small groups, usually family members. Cooperative hunting is more successful than solo hunting and enables capture of larger prey such as jackrabbits. Nest duties often shared between females and males and sometimes by other family members. Young hatch up to a few days apart (asynchronous), leading to young developing at different times. Parents feed the young for up to six months. Produces a second brood in years with abundant food.

Barred Owl
Strix varia

YEAR-ROUND

Size: 20–24" (51–61 cm); up to 3½' wingspan

Male: Chunky brown-and-gray owl. Dark horizontal barring on upper chest. Vertical streaks on lower chest and belly. A large head and dark-brown eyes. Yellow bill and feet.

Female: same as male but slightly larger

Juvenile: light gray with a black face

Nest: cavity; does not add any nesting material; 1 brood per year

Eggs: 2–3; white without markings

Incubation: 28–33 days; female incubates

Fledging: 42–44 days; female and male feed the young

Migration: non-migrator

Food: mice, rabbits and other animals; small birds; fish; reptiles; amphibians

Compare: Great Horned Owl (p. 261) has horns, and the much smaller Eastern Screech-Owl (p. 307) has ears, both of which Barred Owl lacks. Burrowing Owl (p. 187) has long legs and is less than half the size of the Barred Owl. Look for a stocky owl with a large head and dark-brown eyes to identify the Barred Owl.

Stan's Notes: Prefers deciduous woodlands but can be attracted to your yard with a simple nest box that has a large entrance hole. Often seen hunting during the day. Perches and watches for mice, birds and other prey. Hovers over water and reaches down to grab fish. After fledging, the young stay with the parents for up to four months. Often sounds like a dog barking before calling six to eight hoots, sounding like "who-who-who-cooks-for-you."

displaying

Plain Chachalaca
Ortalis vetula

YEAR-ROUND

Size: 21–23" (53–58 cm); up to 2' wingspan

Male: Varying shades of brown with a lighter buff belly and undertail. Small head, long neck and small gray bill. Long, white-tipped dark tail often fans out during flight. Red patch of skin near throat during display.

Female: same as male, but lacks red skin near throat

Juvenile: similar to female

Nest: platform; female builds; 1 brood per year

Eggs: 2–3; cream to white without markings

Incubation: 22–27 days; female incubates

Fledging: 14–21 days; female and male feed young

Migration: non-migrator; moves around to find food

Food: seeds, fruit, insects, leaf buds; will come to ground feeders

Compare: Greater Roadrunner (p. 263) is similar in size, but it is slimmer and has white streaks and a longer bill.

Stan's Notes: A large noisy bird, frequently seen walking on the ground, taking a dust bath or hopping from branch to branch in trees. Glides on short round wings from tree to tree in search of seeds and fruit. Expanded range due to increased backyard bird feeding. Nests in a tree 10–15 feet (3–4.5 m) above ground in a large nest built of large sticks. Young leave nest within hours to a couple days of hatching and follow parents to learn what to eat. Gathers in small groups in late summer and fall and moves to find food. Gives a loud "cha-cha-lac" followed by a group response, "cha-cha-la-ca," which can be heard repeatedly. Name comes from its familiar call.

Great Horned Owl

Bubo virginianus

YEAR-ROUND

Size: 21–25" (53–64 cm); up to 4' wingspan

Male: Robust brown "horned" owl. Bright-yellow eyes and a V-shaped white throat resembling a necklace. Horizontal barring on the chest.

Female: same as male but slightly larger

Juvenile: similar to adults but lacks ear tufts

Nest: no nest; takes over the nest of a crow, hawk or Great Blue Heron or uses a partial cavity, stump or broken tree; 1 brood per year

Eggs: 2–3; white without markings

Incubation: 26–30 days; female incubates

Fledging: 30–35 days; male and female feed the young

Migration: non-migrator

Food: mammals, birds (ducks), snakes, insects

Compare: Burrowing Owl (p. 187) is much smaller and has long legs. Barred Owl (p. 257) has dark eyes and no "horns." The Eastern Screech-Owl (p. 307) is extremely tiny. Look for bright-yellow eyes and feather "horns" on the head to help identify the Great Horned Owl.

Stan's Notes: One of the earliest nesting birds in the state, laying eggs in January and February. Able to hunt in complete darkness due to its excellent hearing. The "horns," or "ears," are tufts of feathers and have nothing to do with hearing. Cannot turn its head all the way around. Wing feathers are ragged on the ends, resulting in silent flight. Eyelids close from the top down, like humans. Fearless, it is one of the few animals that will kill skunks and porcupines. Given that, it is also called the Flying Tiger. Call sounds like "hoo-hoo-hoo-hoooo."

displaying

Greater Roadrunner
Geococcyx californianus

YEAR-ROUND

Size: 23" (58 cm)

Male: Overall brown with white streaking. Long, pointed brown bill. Extremely long tail. Blue patch just behind eyes. Short round wings are darker brown than body. Long gray legs with large feet. Has a conspicuous crest that can be raised and lowered.

Female: same as male

Juvenile: similar to adult

Nest: platform, low in a tree, shrub or cactus; the female and male build; 1–2 broods per year

Eggs: 4–6; white without markings

Incubation: 18–20 days; male and female incubate

Fledging: 16–18 days; male and female feed young

Migration: non-migrator

Food: insects, reptiles, small mammals and birds

Compare: This uniquely shaped ground dweller has an extremely long tail, a prominent crest, and is hard to confuse with other birds.

Stan's Notes: Ground dweller with a very long tail and prominent crest when raised. Cuckoo family member known to run quickly across the ground to catch prey. A formidable predator, able to run up to 15 miles (24 km) per hour. Flies short distances, usually in a low glide after a running takeoff. Raises its tail high, lowers it slowly. A slow, descending, low-pitched "coo-coo-coo-coo." Male does most incubating and feeding of young. Performs a distraction display to protect the nest. Young can catch prey four weeks after leaving the nest.

cinnamon
wing linings

Long-billed Curlew
Numenius americanus

YEAR-ROUND
SUMMER
MIGRATION

Size: 23" (58 cm), including bill

Male: Cinnamon brown with an extremely long, down-curved bill. Long bluish legs. Darker cinnamon wing linings.

Female: same as male, but with a longer bill

Juvenile: same as adults, but with a shorter bill

Nest: ground; female builds; 1 brood per year

Eggs: 5–7; olive-green with brown markings

Incubation: 27–30 days; female and male incubate, the female during day, male at night

Fledging: 32–45 days; female and male feed young

Migration: complete to non-migrator, to coastal Texas, coastal Mexico, Central and South America

Food: insects, worms, crabs, eggs

Compare: Greater Yellowlegs (p. 205) is smaller and lacks the extremely long bill of the Curlew.

Stan's Notes: The largest of shorebirds, with an appropriate name. The extremely long bill is greater than half the length of its body. Female has a longer bill than male. Juvenile has a short bill, which grows into a long bill during the first six months. Uses bill to probe deep into mud for insects and worms. Female incubates during the day, male during the night. Although a shorebird, it is often in grass fields away from the shore. Breeds in open valleys and flatlands. Will fly up to 6 miles (10 km) from nest site to find food. Does not nest in most of Texas, nesting in western states such as Utah, Idaho, Wyoming and Montana. Spends winters along the Gulf Coast.

winter

breeding

in flight

White-faced Ibis
Plegadis chihi

YEAR-ROUND
MIGRATION

Size: 23" (58 cm); up to 3' wingspan

Male: Appears brown with rusty red (chestnut) on upper body. Glossy brown with green sheen on lower body. Long, down-curved gray bill. White border on a light-red face. Orange-red legs and feet. Deep-red eyes. Winter has a gray mask and less chestnut.

Female: same as male

Juvenile: similar to winter adult

Nest: platform, on ground, low in shrub or small tree; female and male build; 1 brood a year

Eggs: 2–4; blue or green with brown markings

Incubation: 21–23 days; female and male incubate

Fledging: 30–35 days; female and male feed young

Migration: complete to non-migrator, to coastal Texas, Mexico

Food: insects, crayfish, frogs, small fish, shellfish

Compare: American Avocet (p. 93) is mostly black and white with an upturned bill.

Stan's Notes: Of the three ibis species in the U.S., this one is seen during migration throughout Texas and year-round along the Gulf Coast. Usually found in marshes and estuaries. When near and in good light, appears glossy red with green, blue and purple highlights. Uses its long bill to find and eat aquatic insects and fish. Large groups fly in a straight line. Rapid, shallow wingbeats, then a short glide. Nests close to the water in large colonies with egrets and herons. Builds a loose nest of thin twigs, leaves and roots, lined with green leaves. Common name comes from the white outline on face.

267

soaring

juvenile

juvenile

Golden Eagle
Aquila chrysaetos

Size: 30–40" (76–102 cm); up to 7¼' wingspan

Male: Uniform dark brown with a golden-yellow head and nape of neck. Yellow around base of bill. Yellow feet.

Female: same as male

Juvenile: similar to adult, with white "wrist" patches and a white base of tail

Nest: platform, on a cliff; female and male build; 1 brood per year

Eggs: 1–2; white with brown markings

Incubation: 43–45 days; female and male incubate

Fledging: 63–75 days; female and male feed young

Migration: non-migrator to partial migrator; moves around to find food

Food: mammals, birds, reptiles, insects

Compare: The Bald Eagle (p. 103) adult is similar, but it has a white head and white tail. Bald Eagle juvenile is often confused with the Golden Eagle juvenile; both are large dark birds with white markings.

Stan's Notes: A large, powerful raptor that has no trouble taking larger prey such as jackrabbits. Hunts by perching or soaring and watching for movement. Inhabits mountainous terrain, requiring large territories to provide a large supply of food. Long-term pair bond, renewing its bond late in winter with spectacular high-flying courtship displays. Usually nests on cliff faces; rarely nests in trees. Uses a well-established nest that's been used for generations. Will add items to the nest such as antlers, bones and barbed wire.

displaying male

non-displaying

female

Wild Turkey

Meleagris gallopavo

YEAR-ROUND

Size: 36–48" (91–122 cm)

Male: Large brown-and-bronze bird with a naked blue-and-red head. Long, straight, black beard in the center of the chest. Tail spreads open like a fan. Spurs on legs.

Female: thinner and less striking than the male; often lacks a breast beard

Juvenile: same as adult of the same sex

Nest: ground; female builds; 1 brood per year

Eggs: 10–12; buff-white with dull-brown markings

Incubation: 27–28 days; female incubates

Fledging: 6–10 days; female leads the young to food

Migration: non-migrator; moves around to find food

Food: insects, seeds, fruit

Compare: This bird is quite distinctive and unlikely to be confused with others.

Stan's Notes: The largest native game bird in Texas, and the species from which the domestic turkey was bred. A strong flier that can approach 60 miles (97 km) per hour. Can fly straight up, then away. Eyesight is three times better than ours. Hearing is also excellent; can hear competing males up to a mile away. Male has a "harem" of up to 20 females. Female scrapes out a shallow depression for nesting and pads it with soft leaves. Males are known as toms, females are hens, and young are poults. Roosts in trees at night. Eliminated from many of the eastern states by the turn of the 20th century due to market hunting and loss of habitat, and reintroduced in the 1960–80s. Populations are now stable.

juvenile

breeding

non-breeding

chick-feeding adult

Brown Pelican
Pelecanus occidentalis

YEAR-ROUND

Size: 46–50" (117–127 cm); up to 7' wingspan

Male: Gray-brown body, black belly, exceptionally long gray bill. Breeding adult has a white or yellow head with dark chestnut hind neck. Adult that is feeding chicks (chick-feeding adult) has a speckled white head. A non-breeding adult has a white head and neck.

Female: similar to male

Juvenile: brown with white breast and belly; does not acquire adult plumage until the third year

Nest: ground; female and male build; 1 brood per year

Eggs: 2–4; white without markings

Incubation: 28–30 days; female and male incubate

Fledging: 71–86 days; female and male feed the young

Migration: non-migrator

Food: fish

Compare: American White Pelican (p. 411) is similar, but it is white with a bright-yellow or orange bill.

Stan's Notes: A coastal bird of Texas and recently was an endangered species. Suffering from eggshell thinning in the 1970s due to DDT and other pesticides, it is now reestablishing along the East, Gulf and West Coasts. Captures fish by diving headfirst into the ocean, opening its large bill and "netting" fish with its gular pouch. Often seen sitting on posts around marinas. Nests in large colonies. Doesn't breed before the age of 3, when it obtains its breeding plumage.

Ruby-crowned Kinglet
Regulus calendula

WINTER

Size: 4" (10 cm)

Male: Small, teardrop-shaped green-to-gray bird. Two white wing bars and a white eye-ring. Hidden ruby crown.

Female: same as male, but lacks a ruby crown

Juvenile: same as female

Nest: pendulous; female builds; 1 brood per year

Eggs: 4–5; white with brown markings

Incubation: 11–12 days; female incubates

Fledging: 11–12 days; female and male feed the young

Migration: complete, to Texas and Mexico

Food: insects, berries

Compare: The female American Goldfinch (p. 415) shares the drab olive plumage and unmarked chest, but it is larger. Look for the white eye-ring to identify the Ruby-crowned Kinglet.

Stan's Notes: This is one of the smaller birds in the state. Most commonly seen during migration. Look for it flitting around thick shrubs low to the ground. It takes a quick eye to see the ruby crown, which the male flashes when he is excited. The female weaves an unusually intricate nest and fastens colorful lichens and mosses to the exterior with spiderwebs. Often builds the nest high in a mature tree, where it hangs from a branch that has overlapping leaves. Sings a distinctive song that starts out soft and ends loud and on a higher note. "Kinglet" originates from the word *king*, referring to the male's red crown, and the diminutive suffix *let*, meaning "small." A winter resident throughout Texas.

male

female

WINTER

Red-breasted Nuthatch
Sitta canadensis

Size: 4½" (11 cm)

Male: Gray-backed bird with an obvious black eye line and black cap. Rust-red breast and belly.

Female: duller than male and has a gray cap and pale undersides

Juvenile: same as female

Nest: cavity; male and female excavate a cavity or move into a vacant hole; 1 brood per year

Eggs: 5–6; white with red brown markings

Incubation: 11–12 days; female incubates

Fledging: 14–20 days; female and male feed the young

Migration: irruptive; moves around the state in search of food

Food: insects, insect eggs, seeds; comes to seed and suet feeders

Compare: The White-breasted Nuthatch (p. 285) is larger and has a white breast. Look for the rust-red breast and black eye line to help identify the Red-breasted Nuthatch.

Stan's Notes: The nuthatch climbs down trunks of trees headfirst, searching for insects. Like a chickadee, it grabs a seed from a feeder and flies off to crack it open. Wedges the seed into a crevice and pounds it open with several sharp blows. The name "Nuthatch" comes from the Middle English moniker *nuthak*, referring to the habit of hacking seeds open. Look for it in mature conifers, where it extracts seeds from pine cones. Excavates a cavity or takes an old woodpecker hole or a natural cavity and builds a nest within. An irruptive migrator, common in some winters and scarce in others. Gives a series of nasal "yank-yank-yank" calls.

male

juvenile

female

YEAR-ROUND

Verdin
Auriparus flaviceps

Size: 4½" (11 cm)

Male: Light gray to silvery overall. Lemon-yellow head. Rusty-red shoulder patch, frequently hidden. Short, pointed dark bill. Dark mark between bill and eyes. Dark legs and feet.

Female: duller than male

Juvenile: overall gray, lacks the yellow head, dark bill and rusty-red shoulder patch

Nest: covered cup; male builds; 1–2 broods a year

Eggs: 4–5; bluish green with brown markings

Incubation: 8–10 days; female incubates

Fledging: 19–21 days; female and male feed young

Migration: non-migrator

Food: seeds, insects, fruit, nectar; comes to nectar feeders and orange halves

Compare: Smaller than the Tufted Titmouse (p. 291), which has a crest and lacks a yellow head.

Stan's Notes: A very friendly bird that can be a regular visitor to nectar feeders and orange halves. Often hides its rusty-red shoulder marks, confusing the novice bird watcher. Most easily identified as a tiny gray bird with a yellow head. Male builds several ball-shaped, conspicuous nests of thorny twigs, interweaves them with leaves and grass and lines them with feathers and plant down. Male shows the nest possibilities to female and she selects one. After fledging, young return to nest at night unlike most small birds, which leave and don't return for shelter. Often uses nest for several seasons.

Carolina Chickadee

Poecile carolinensis

YEAR-ROUND

Size: 5" (13 cm)

Male: Mostly gray with a black cap and chin. White face and chest with a tan belly. Darker-gray tail.

Female: same as male

Juvenile: same as adult

Nest: cavity; female and male build or excavate; 1–2 broods per year

Eggs: 5–7; white with reddish brown markings

Incubation: 11–12 days; female and male incubate

Fledging: 13–17 days; female and male feed the young

Migration: non-migrator

Food: insects, seeds, fruit; comes to seed and suet feeders

Compare: Tufted Titmouse and Black-crested Titmouse (p. 291) are close relatives, but they have an erect crest and lack the black cap and chin.

Stan's Notes: One of the first birds to use a newly placed feeder. Flies to a feeder, grabs a seed and carries it to a branch. To get to the meat inside, it holds the seed down with its feet and hammers the shell open with its bill. Returns for another seed. A friendly bird. Can be tamed and hand fed. Attracted with a nest box that has a 1¼-inch entrance hole. Female gives a loud snake-like hiss if disturbed on the nest. Often seen with other birds (mixed flock) in winter. Song is a high, fast "chika-dee-dee-dee-dee."

female
p. 145

male

pink-sided

Oregon
male

Dark-eyed Junco
Junco hyemalis

WINTER

Size: 5½" (14 cm)

Male: Plump, dark-eyed bird with a slate-gray-to-charcoal chest, head and back. White belly. Pink bill. White outer tail feathers appear like a white V in flight.

Female: round with brown plumage

Juvenile: similar to female, with streaking on the breast and head

Nest: cup; female and male build; 2 broods per year

Eggs: 3–5; white with reddish brown markings

Incubation: 12–13 days; female incubates

Fledging: 10–13 days; male and female feed the young

Migration: complete, to Texas

Food: seeds, insects; visits ground and seed feeders

Compare: Rarely confused with any other bird. Look for the pink bill and small flocks feeding under feeders to identify the male Dark-eyed Junco.

Stan's Notes: Several junco species have now been combined into one, simply called Dark-eyed Junco (see lower insets). Nests in a wide variety of wooded habitats in April and May. Adheres to a rigid social hierarchy, with dominant birds chasing the less dominant ones. Look for the white outer tail feathers flashing in flight. Often seen in small flocks on the ground, where it uses its feet to simultaneously "double-scratch" to expose seeds and insects. Eats many weed seeds. Males don't go as far south as females in winter. Doesn't nest in Texas.

male

female

White-breasted Nuthatch

Sitta carolinensis

YEAR-ROUND
WINTER

Size: 5–6" (13–15 cm)

Male: Slate gray with a white face, breast and belly. Large white patch on the rump. Black cap and nape. Bill is long and thin, slightly upturned. Chestnut undertail.

Female: similar to male, but has a gray cap and nape

Juvenile: similar to female

Nest: cavity; female and male build a nest within; 1 brood per year

Eggs: 5–7; white with brown markings

Incubation: 11–12 days; female incubates

Fledging: 13–14 days; female and male feed the young

Migration: non-migrator

Food: insects, insect eggs, seeds; comes to seed and suet feeders

Compare: Red-breasted Nuthatch (p. 277) is smaller and has a rust-red belly and distinctive black eye line. Look for the white breast to help identify the White-breasted Nuthatch.

Stan's Notes: The nuthatch hops headfirst down trees, looking for insects missed by birds climbing up. Its climbing agility is due to an extra-long hind toe claw, or nail, that is nearly twice the size of its front claws. "Nuthatch," from the Middle English *nuthak*, refers to the bird's habit of wedging a seed in a crevice and hacking it open. Often seen in flocks with chickadees and Downy Woodpeckers. Mates stay together year-round, defending a small territory. Gives a characteristic "whi-whi-whi-whi" spring call during February to May. One of nearly 30 worldwide nuthatch species.

male

female

first
winter

Yellow-rumped Warbler
Setophaga coronata

YEAR-ROUND
WINTER

Size: 5–6" (13–15 cm)

Male: Slate gray with black streaking on the chest. Yellow patches on the head, flanks and rump. White chin and belly. Two white wing bars.

Female: duller gray than the male, mixed with brown

Juvenile: first winter is similar to the adult female

Nest: cup; female builds; 2 broods per year

Eggs: 4–5; white with brown markings

Incubation: 12–13 days; female incubates

Fledging: 10–12 days; female and male feed young

Migration: partial migrator to non-migrator in Texas

Food: insects, berries; visits suet feeders in spring

Compare: The male Wilson's Warbler (p. 417) has a black cap. The male Common Yellowthroat (p. 419) has a yellow chest and distinctive black mask. Look for patches of yellow on the rump, head, flanks and chin of Yellow-rumped Warbler to help identify.

Stan's Notes: A common warbler in Texas. Flocks of hundreds are seen when northern birds join residents for the winter. Familiar call is a single robust "chip," heard mostly during migration. Sings a wonderful song in spring. Usually arrives in late September to early October. Moves quickly among trees and from the ground to trees. Flits around the upper branches of tall trees. In the fall, the male molts to a dull color similar to the female, but he retains his yellow patches all year. Frequently called Myrtle Warbler in eastern states and Audubon's Warbler in western states. Sometimes called Butter-butt due to the yellow patch on its rump.

287

Black-throated Sparrow
Amphispiza bilineata

YEAR-ROUND

Size: 6" (15 cm)

Male: Overall smooth gray bird with bold black-and-white markings on head and face. Large black patch on the throat. Darker-gray tail with white edges.

Female: same as male

Juvenile: similar to adult, lacks the black-and-white head pattern and black throat

Nest: cup; female builds; 1–2 broods per year

Eggs: 3–4; pale blue to white without markings

Incubation: 12–14 days; female incubates

Fledging: 10–12 days; female and male feed young

Migration: non-migrator in Texas

Food: insects, seeds, leaf buds

Compare: Breeding male Lark Bunting (p. 59) is black with white wing patches. Female and non-breeding male Lark Buntings (p. 157) have heavily streaked breasts. Look for the black throat patch to identify the Black-throated Sparrow.

Stan's Notes: A sparrow of desert scrub and rocky uplands. Male often perches on prominent spots in its territory and sings a short, simple, tinkling song or a high, bell-like "tee-tee-tee." Often holds off breeding until rainfall produces enough food. Female constructs a cup nest of dried grass low in a cactus and lines it with finer plant materials. Although the young are fed a diet of insects, adults will eat new green shoots of trees, shrubs and grasses along with insects and seeds. Forms small flocks in the winter of up to 20 individuals, often with other sparrow species.

Black-crested
Titmouse

Tufted Titmouse

Baeolophus bicolor

YEAR-ROUND

Size: 6" (15 cm)

Male: Slate gray with a white chest and belly. Pointed crest. Rust-brown wash on the flanks. Gray legs and dark eyes.

Female: same as male

Juvenile: same as adult

Nest: cavity; female lines an old woodpecker cavity; 2 broods per year

Eggs: 5–7; white with brown markings

Incubation: 13–14 days; female incubates

Fledging: 15–18 days; female and male feed the young

Migration: non-migrator

Food: insects, seeds, fruit; will come to seed and suet feeders

Compare: The Carolina Chickadee (p. 281) is a close relative but is smaller and lacks a crest. White-breasted Nuthatch (p. 285) is a similar size and color but lacks a crest.

Stan's Notes: A common feeder bird that can be attracted with an offering of black oil sunflower seeds or suet. Well known for its "peter-peter-peter" call, which it quickly repeats. Notorious for pulling hair from sleeping dogs, cats and squirrels to line its nest. Usually seen only one or two at a time. The prefix *tit* in the common name comes from a Scandinavian word meaning "little." Suffix *mouse* is derived from the Old English word *mase*, meaning "bird." Simply translated, it is a "small bird." The Black-crested Titmouse (see inset) occurs in central and southern parts of the state. Map reflects the combined range. Hybridization results in birds with dark gray crests and pale foreheads.

291

breeding
p. 155

winter

Least Sandpiper
Calidris minutilla

YEAR-ROUND
MIGRATION
WINTER

Size: 6" (15 cm)

Male: Winter plumage is overall gray to light brown, with a distinct brown breast band and white belly. Light-gray eyebrows and short, thin, down-curved black bill. Dull-yellow legs.

Female: same as male

Juvenile: similar to winter adult, but buff-brown and lacks the breast band

Nest: ground; male and female construct; 1 brood per year

Eggs: 3–4; olive with dark markings

Incubation: 19–23 days; male and female incubate

Fledging: 25–28 days; male and female feed the young

Migration: complete to non-migrator, to Texas, Mexico and Central America

Food: aquatic and terrestrial insects, seeds

Compare: The smallest of sandpipers. Least Sandpiper's yellow legs differentiate it from other tiny sandpipers. Look for the short, thin, down-curved bill to help identify.

Stan's Notes: Winters in southern coastal states from the Carolinas to California. This is a tiny, tame sandpiper that can be approached without scaring it. It is the smallest of peeps (sandpipers), nesting on the tundra in northern regions of Canada and Alaska. Prefers the grassy flats of saltwater and freshwater ponds. Its yellow legs can be hard to see in water, poor light or when covered with mud. Most other small shorebirds have black legs and feet.

female

male p. 381

Vermilion Flycatcher

Pyrocephalus rubinus

Size: 6" (15 cm)

Female: A mostly gray bird with a gray head, neck and back. Nearly white chin and chest. Pink belly to undertail. Black tail. Thin black bill.

Male: crimson-red head, crest, chin, breast and belly, black nape of neck, back, wings and tail, black line through eyes, thin black bill

Juvenile: similar to female, lacks a pink undertail

Nest: cup; female builds; 1–2 broods per year

Eggs: 2–4; white with brown markings

Incubation: 14–16 days; female and male incubate

Fledging: 14–16 days; female and male feed young

Migration: complete, to Mexico

Food: insects (mainly bees)

Compare: The phoebes (p. 65, p. 297) of Texas have a similar body and bill shape and share a similar habitat. Black Phoebe (p. 65) is black with a white belly.

Stan's Notes: A summer resident with few staying all winter in extreme southern Texas. Often in open areas with shrubs and small trees close to water. Will perch on a thin branch, pumping tail up and down while waiting for an aerial insect. Flies out to snatch it, then returns to perch. Drops to the ground for terrestrial insects. Male raises its crest, fluffs chest feathers, fans tail and sings a song during a fluttery flight to court females. Female builds a shallow nest of twigs and grasses and lines it with downy plant material. Male feeds female during incubation and brooding.

Eastern Phoebe
Sayornis phoebe

YEAR-ROUND
SUMMER
WINTER

Size: 6½" (18 cm)

Male: Plain gray with slightly darker wings, a light-olive belly and a thin, dark bill.

Female: same as male

Juvenile: same as adults

Nest: cup; female builds; 2 broods per year

Eggs: 4–5; white without markings

Incubation: 15–16 days; female incubates

Fledging: 15–16 days; male and female feed the young

Migration: complete, to southern Texas and Mexico, non-migrator in eastern parts of Texas

Food: insects

Compare: The Gray Catbird (p. 309) has a black crown and a chestnut patch under its tail. Eastern Phoebe lacks any distinctive markings. Listen for its well-enunciated "fee-bee" call and look for the hawking and tail-pumping behaviors to help identify this bird.

Stan's Notes: A sparrow-size bird that often perches on the end of a dead branch. Found in forests, yards and farms. In a process called hawking, it waits for a passing insect. When a bug flies near, it launches out to catch it and then returns to the same branch. It has a distinctive habit of pumping its tail up and down while perching. Builds nest beneath the eaves of houses, under bridges or in other sheltered spots. Uses mud, grass and moss for nest materials and hair (and sometimes feathers) for the lining. The common name is derived from its distinctive "fee-bee" call, which it repeats over and over from the top of dead branches.

Common Ground-Dove

Columbina passerina

YEAR-ROUND

Size: 6½" (16 cm)

Male: A very small dove with a short tail and a unique scalloped appearance on head and chest. Black-tipped reddish-orange bill and slate-gray crown. Pinkish-gray underside. Bright-chestnut wing linings, seen in flight.

Female: similar to male, but grayer and has a more uniform color

Juvenile: similar to adult

Nest: ground; female and male build; 2–4 broods per year

Eggs: 2–4; white without markings

Incubation: 12–14 days; female and male incubate

Fledging: 10–11 days; female and male feed young

Migration: non-migrator

Food: seeds, berries; will come to seed feeders

Compare: The Mourning Dove (p. 199) is twice the size of Common Ground-Dove and lacks the scalloped appearance and chestnut-colored wing linings.

Stan's Notes: The smallest dove in Texas, formerly called Eastern Ground Dove. Known to continually bob its head. Frequently seen in pairs. Unafraid of humans and spends most of its time on the ground. While it usually nests on the ground, it sometimes builds a flimsy nest in a shrub or takes an abandoned nest low in a tree. Seen in open dry woodlands, old fields and pastures. Walks around with mechanical movements, bobbing its head and shuffling its feet like a wind-up toy.

YEAR-ROUND

Inca Dove
Columbina inca

Size: 8" (20 cm)

Male: A small thin-bodied dove, pale gray overall. Scalloped or scaly appearance due to dark-edged feathers. Lighter gray head. Dark thin bill. Dark-red eyes. Long thin tail. White outer tail feathers and dark rusty wing linings, seen in flight.

Female: same as male

Juvenile: similar to adult, lacks a scaly pattern

Nest: platform; female and male build; 2–3 broods per year

Eggs: 2; white without markings

Incubation: 12–14 days; female and male incubate

Fledging: 14–16 days; female and male feed young

Migration: non-migrator

Food: seeds, fruit; visits seed feeders on ground

Compare: One of the smallest doves in Texas. Scaly appearance assures correct identification.

Stan's Notes: Seen in many habitats, including cities and suburbs, mostly in arid areas with some low scrubby growth. Male bows to female with tail fanned to show white sides. Outer wing feathers produce a buzzing sound in flight. Groups of up to 50 birds gather in summer and winter to find food. Roosts in large groups, sitting side by side or sometimes one on another. Huddles in "pyramids," sometimes stacked two or three individuals high. Constructs a loose platform nest of twigs, grass and leaves. Nest is sometimes built on the ground, low in a tree or shrub or in a hanging flower basket. Will also reuse the nest of larger doves, such as Mourning Doves.

Eastern Kingbird

Tyrannus tyrannus

SUMMER
MIGRATION

Size: 8" (20 cm)

Male: Mostly gray and black with a white chin and belly. Black head and tail with a distinct white band on the tip of the tail. Concealed red crown, rarely seen.

Female: same as male

Juvenile: same as adults

Nest: cup; male and female build; 1 brood per year

Eggs: 3–4; white with brown markings

Incubation: 16–18 days; female incubates

Fledging: 16–18 days; female and male feed the young

Migration: complete, to Mexico, Central America and South America

Food: insects, fruit

Compare: American Robin (p. 315) is larger and has a rust-red breast. Western Kingbird (p. 437) is yellow on the belly and under the wings. The Eastern Phoebe (p. 297) is smaller and has an olive-green belly.

Stan's Notes: Found in open fields and prairies. As many as 20 birds migrate in a group. Returns to the mating ground in spring, where pairs defend their territory. Seems to be unafraid of other birds and chases larger birds. Given the common name "King" for its bold attitude and behavior. In a hunting technique known as hawking, it perches on a branch and watches for insects, flies out to catch one, and then returns to the same perch. Swoops from perch to perch when hunting. Becomes very vocal during late summer, when family members call back and forth to one another while hunting for insects.

breeding
p. 175

winter

Sanderling
Calidris alba

YEAR-ROUND
MIGRATION

Size: 8" (20 cm)

Male: The lightest sandpiper on the beach during winter. Winter plumage has gray head and back and white belly. Black legs and bill. White wing stripe, seen only in flight.

Female: same as male

Juvenile: spotty black on the head and back with a white belly; black legs and bill

Nest: ground; male builds; 1–2 broods per year

Eggs: 3–4; greenish olive with brown markings

Incubation: 24–30 days; male and female incubate

Fledging: 16–17 days; female and male feed the young

Migration: complete, to non-migrator, to coastal Texas, Mexico, Central America and South America

Food: insects

Compare: Winter Spotted Sandpiper (p. 173) is the same size but lacks black legs and an all-black bill. Winter Black-bellied Plover (p. 323) has a similar color but is much larger with a larger bill.

Stan's Notes: One of the most common shorebirds in Texas, but mostly seen in its gray winter plumage from August to April. Seen in groups on sandy beaches, running out with each retreating wave to feed. Look for a flash of white on the wings when it is in flight. Both sexes perform a distraction display if threatened. Nests on the Arctic Tundra. Rests by standing on one leg and tucking the other into its belly feathers. Often hops away on one leg, moving away from pedestrians on the beach. Surveys show a large decline in numbers since the 1970s.

red morph

gray morph

Eastern Screech-Owl

Megascops asio

YEAR-ROUND

Size: 8–10" (20–25 cm); up to 2' wingspan

Male: Small "eared" owl that occurs in different colorations. Gray morph is mottled gray and white. Red morph is mottled rust and white. Short wings. Bright-yellow eyes.

Female: same as male but slightly larger

Juvenile: lighter color than adults of the same morph and usually lacks ear tufts

Nest: cavity, old woodpecker cavity or man-made nest box; does not add any nesting material; 1 brood per year

Eggs: 4–5; white without markings

Incubation: 25–26 days; female incubates, male feeds the female during incubation

Fledging: 26–27 days; male and female feed the young

Migration: non-migrator; moves around in winter

Food: large insects, small mammals, birds, snakes

Compare: Burrowing Owl (p. 187) is slightly larger and lacks ear tufts. Eastern Screech-Owl is hard to confuse with its considerably larger cousin, the Great Horned Owl (p. 261).

Stan's Notes: Commonly found in areas that have suitable natural cavities for nesting and roosting. Active from dusk to dawn. Usually gives a tremulous, descending trill, like a sound effect in a scary movie. Seldom gives a screeching call. Often seen sunning itself at a nest-box hole during winter. Mates may have a long-term pair bond and may roost together at night. Excellent hearing and eyesight. Flaps rapidly and flies silently. Has winter and summer territories. The gray morph is more common than the red.

Gray Catbird
Dumetella carolinensis

SUMMER
MIGRATION
WINTER

Size: 9" (22.5 cm)

Male: Handsome slate-gray bird with a black crown and a long, thin, black bill. Often lifts up its tail, exposing a chestnut patch beneath.

Female: same as male

Juvenile: same as adults

Nest: cup; female and male build; 2 broods per year

Eggs: 4–6; blue-green without markings

Incubation: 12–13 days; female incubates

Fledging: 10–11 days; female and male feed young

Migration: complete to non-migrator, to eastern Texas

Food: insects, occasional fruit; visits suet feeders

Compare: The Eastern Phoebe (p. 297) is smaller and has an olive belly. The Eastern Kingbird (p. 303) is similar in size but has a white belly and a white band across its tail. To identify the Gray Catbird, look for the black crown and chestnut patch under the tail.

Stan's Notes: A secretive bird, more often heard than seen. The Chippewa Indians gave it a name that means "the bird that cries with grief" due to its raspy call. Called "Catbird" because the sound is like the meowing of a house cat. Often mimics other birds, rarely repeating the same phrases. Found in forest edges, backyards and parks. Builds its nest with small twigs. Nests in thick shrubs and quickly flies back into shrubs if approached. If a cowbird lays an egg in its nest, the catbird will quickly break it and eject it.

male

female

Pyrrhuloxia
Cardinalis sinuatus

YEAR-ROUND

Size: 9" (22.5 cm)

Male: Overall gray with a red mask, throat, breast and belly. Red edges of wings and tail. Bright-red-tipped crest. Stout yellow bill. Dark eyes.

Female: similar to male, lacking red on face, throat, breast and belly, bill is gray to dull yellow

Juvenile: similar to female, has a dark gray bill, lacks red highlights

Nest: cup; female builds; 1 brood per year

Eggs: 2–4; gray to green with brown markings

Incubation: 12–14 days; female and male incubate

Fledging: 8–10 days; female and male feed young

Migration: non-migrator

Food: seeds, fruit, insects; will visit water elements and ground feeders

Compare: Female Northern Cardinal (p. 177) has a black mask and a pointed red bill. Look for the Pyrrhuloxia's tall crest and long tail.

Stan's Notes: This is a secretive bird of arid brush, thorn scrub and mesquite habitat. Like its cousin, the Northern Cardinal, it is most active in early morning and just before sunset. Has a similar loud, crisp song like the cardinal and a single metallic "chip" call. Small flocks move around in the winter to find food. Feeds mostly on the ground, eating grass seeds and insects. Male feeds female during courtship and incubation. Female constructs a nest with twigs and grass in dense shrubs or thickets and lines it with fine grasses and plant fibers. Both defend home territory during the breeding season. Use water elements and ground feeders to attract it to your yard.

311

Loggerhead Shrike
Lanius ludovicianus

YEAR-ROUND

Size: 9" (22.5 cm)

Male: Gray head and back and a white chin, breast and belly. Black wings, tail, legs and feet. Black mask across the eyes and a black bill with a hooked tip. White wing patches, seen in flight.

Female: same as male

Juvenile: dull version of adult

Nest: cup; male and female construct; 1–2 broods per year

Eggs: 4–7; off-white with dark markings

Incubation: 16–17 days; female incubates

Fledging: 17–21 days; female and male feed the young

Migration: non-migrator in Texas

Food: insects, lizards, small mammals, frogs

Compare: The Northern Mockingbird (p. 317) has a similar color pattern, but it lacks the black mask. The Cedar Waxwing (p. 167) has a black mask, but it is a brown bird, not gray and black like the Loggerhead Shrike.

Stan's Notes: The Loggerhead is a songbird that acts like a bird of prey. Known for skewering prey on barbed wire fences, thorns and other sharp objects to store or hold still while tearing apart to eat, hence its other common name, Butcher Bird. Feet are too weak to hold the prey it eats. Breeding bird surveys indicate declining populations in the Great Plains due to pesticides killing its major food source—grasshoppers.

American Robin
Turdus migratorius

YEAR-ROUND
WINTER

Size: 9–11" (23–28 cm)

Male: Familiar gray bird with a dark rust-red breast and a nearly black head and tail. White chin with black streaks. White eye-ring.

Female: similar to male, with a duller rust-red breast and a gray head

Juvenile: similar to female, with a speckled breast and brown back

Nest: cup; female builds with help from the male; 2–3 broods per year

Eggs: 4–7; pale blue without markings

Incubation: 12–14 days; female incubates

Fledging: 14–16 days; female and male feed the young

Migration: non-migrator to complete in Texas

Food: insects, fruit, berries, earthworms

Compare: Familiar bird to all. To differentiate the male from the female, compare the nearly black head and rust-red chest of the male with the gray head and duller chest of the female.

Stan's Notes: The robin is a complete migrator in northern states, but in Texas it is only a complete migrator in half of the state and a year-round resident in the other. Northern birds join resident birds in the state during winter, increasing the population. City robins sing louder than country robins in order to hear one another over traffic and noise. A robin isn't listening for worms when it turns its head to one side. It is focusing its sight out of one eye to look for dirt moving, which is caused by worms moving. Territorial, often fighting its reflection in a window. Males have dark heads and a brighter red breast than females.

displaying

Northern Mockingbird
Mimus polyglottos

YEAR-ROUND

Size: 10" (25 cm)

Male: Silvery-gray head and back with a light-gray breast and belly. White wing patches, seen in flight or during display. Tail mostly black with white outer tail feathers. Black bill.

Female: same as male

Juvenile: dull gray with a heavily streaked breast and a gray bill

Nest: cup; female and male construct; 2 broods per year, sometimes more

Eggs: 3–5; blue-green with brown markings

Incubation: 12–13 days; female incubates

Fledging: 11–13 days; female and male feed the young

Migration: non-migrator in Texas

Food: insects, fruit

Compare: Loggerhead Shrike (p. 313) has a similar color pattern, but it is stockier, has a black mask and perches in more-open places. The Gray Catbird (p. 309) is slate gray and lacks wing patches.

Stan's Notes: A very animated bird. Performs an elaborate mating dance. Facing each other with heads and tails erect, pairs will run toward each other, flashing their white wing patches, and then retreat to cover nearby. Thought to flash the wing patches to scare up insects when hunting. Sits for long periods on top of shrubs. Imitates other birds (vocal mimicry); hence the common name. Young males often sing at night. Often unafraid of people, allowing for close observation.

Curve-billed Thrasher

Toxostoma curvirostre

YEAR-ROUND

Size: 11" (28 cm)

Male: Overall gray to light-brown large-bodied bird with a long tail. Faint spots on breast and belly. Long downward-curved bill. Dark-yellow-to-orange eyes.

Female: same as male

Juvenile: similar to adult, with a shorter bill

Nest: cup; female and male construct; 1–2 broods per year

Eggs: 3–4; pale blue-green with brown markings

Incubation: 12–14 days; female and male incubate

Fledging: 14–18 days; female and male feed young

Migration: non-migrator

Food: insects, fruit, seeds; comes to seed feeders on the ground and water elements

Compare: Brown Thrasher (p. 195) is rusty red with dark spots on the chest. Cactus Wren (p. 179) is smaller and has a spotty dark patch on the chest and a chestnut-brown cap.

Stan's Notes: A familiar backyard bird that prefers scrubby desert habitat with mesquite, cholla and other cactus. Will drive out any Cactus Wrens in its territory. Calls a loud, two-syllable "whit-wee." Feeds on the ground. Male follows female during courtship, singing a soft song. Builds nest in a spiny shrub or cactus, using twigs and grass and lining it with finer plant material. Will often reuse the nest after making minor repairs. Pairs often remain together all year. Young hatch on sequential days, requiring the parents to brood young for more than two weeks. In hot weather parents shade the young from sun.

White-winged Dove
Zenaida asiatica

YEAR-ROUND
SUMMER

Size: 11" (28 cm)

Male: Light-gray-to-brown dove. A conspicuous white edge on the wings. Small black dash underneath the cheeks. Vivid blue eye-rings around bright-red eyes. Black wing tips with a white patch across the middle of wings, as seen in flight.

Female: same as male

Juvenile: similar to adult

Nest: platform; female and male build; 2–3 broods per year

Eggs: 2–4; white without markings

Incubation: 13–14 days; female and male incubate

Fledging: 13–16 days; female and male feed young

Migration: partial migrator to non-migrator

Food: seeds, fruit; will come to seed feeders

Compare: Mourning Dove (p. 199) is slightly larger and lacks the white line on closed wings and a white-and-black pattern in flight.

Stan's Notes: Very similar to the Mourning Dove in behavior and appearance. Feeds on the ground, pecking at seeds and tiny grains of rock to aid digestion. Parents feed young a regurgitated liquid called crop-milk the first few days of life. Male uses its white-and-black wing coloration to display to mate. May nest alone or in large colonies. Gives a distinctive call, "coo-cuk-ca-roo."

breeding
p. 79

winter

Black-bellied Plover
Pluvialis squatarola

YEAR-ROUND MIGRATION

Size: 11–12" (28–30 cm)

Male: Winter plumage is uniform light gray with a white belly and breast. Faint white eyebrow mark. Black legs and bill.

Female: less black on belly and breast than male

Juvenile: grayer than adults, with much less black

Nest: ground; male and female construct; 1 brood per year

Eggs: 3–4; pinkish or greenish with black-brown markings

Incubation: 26–27 days; male incubates during the day, female incubates at night

Fledging: 35–45 days; male feeds the young, the young learn quickly to feed themselves

Migration: complete to non-migrator, to coastal Texas, Mexico, Central America and South America

Food: insects

Compare: The Winter Sanderling (p. 305) has a smaller bill. Winter Spotted Sandpiper (p. 173) has a shorter, thicker bill.

Stan's Notes: Males perform a "butterfly" courtship flight to attract females. Female leaves male and young about 12 days after the eggs hatch. Breeds at age 3. A common year-round resident along the coast. Begins arriving in July and August (fall migration) and leaves in April. During flight, in any plumage, displays a white rump and stripe on wings with black axillaries (armpits). Often darts across the ground to grab an insect and run.

soaring

juvenile

Sharp-shinned Hawk

Accipiter striatus

MIGRATION WINTER

Size: 10–14" (25–36 cm); up to 2' wingspan

Male: Small woodland hawk with a gray back and head and a rust-red chest. Short wings. Long, squared tail and several dark tail bands, with the widest at the end of the tail. Red eyes.

Female: same as male but larger

Juvenile: same size as adults, with a brown back, heavy streaking on the chest and yellow eyes

Nest: platform; female builds; 1 brood per year

Eggs: 4–5; white with brown markings

Incubation: 32–35 days; female incubates

Fledging: 24–27 days; female and male feed the young

Migration: complete, to Texas

Food: birds, small mammals

Compare: Cooper's Hawk (p. 335) is larger and has a larger head, a slightly longer neck and a rounded tail. Red-shouldered Hawk (p. 221) is larger, has a reddish head and belly. Look for the squared tail to help identify the Sharp-shinned Hawk.

Stan's Notes: A hawk of backyards, parks and woodlands. Seen swooping on birds visiting feeders and chasing them as they flee. Its short wingspan and long tail help it to maneuver through thick stands of trees in pursuit of prey. Calls a loud, high-pitched "kik-kik-kik-kik." Named "Sharp-shinned" for the sharp projection (keel) on the leading edge of its shin. A bird's shin is actually below the ankle (rather than above it, like ours) on the tarsus bone of its foot. In most birds, the tarsus bone is rounded, not sharp.

soaring

juvenile

soaring
juvenile

Mississippi Kite
Ictinia mississippiensis

SUMMER
MIGRATION

Size: 12–15" (30–38 cm); up to 2¾' wingspan

Male: Overall gray bird with a paler, nearly white head. Nearly black tail. Dark eye patch surrounding red eyes. Short, hooked gray bill. Yellow legs and feet.

Female: same as male

Juvenile: similar to adult but has a brown chest with vertical white streaks

Nest: platform; female and male build; 1 brood per year

Eggs: 1–2; white without markings

Incubation: 29–32 days; female and male incubate

Fledging: 32–34 days; female and male feed young

Migration: complete, to South America

Food: insects, lizards, small snakes

Compare: Smaller than many other birds of prey. The overall gray appearance with a lighter head makes it easy to identify.

Stan's Notes: A bird of prey that eats mostly large insects. Groups follow livestock, feeding on insects they kick up. Hunts insects by soaring or hovering, catching in flight or diving down. It requires open areas with scattered trees for nesting. Nests in semi-colonies. Mated pairs aggressively defend nest sites. Individuals often stray out of traditional ranges, appearing in northern states and up the East Coast.

Eurasian Collared-Dove
Streptopelia decaocto

YEAR-ROUND

Size: 12½" (32 cm)

Male: Head, neck, breast and belly are gray to tan. Back, wings and tail are slightly darker. Thin black collar with a white border on the nape of the neck. Tail is long and squared.

Female: same as male

Juvenile: similar to adults

Nest: platform; female and male build; 2–3 broods per year

Eggs: 3–5; creamy white without markings

Incubation: 12–14 days; female and male incubate

Fledging: 12–14 days; female and male feed the young

Migration: non-migrator

Food: seeds; will visit ground and seed feeders

Compare: The Mourning Dove (p. 199) is slightly smaller and darker. The Rock Pigeon (p. 331) has colorful iridescent patches. Look for the black collar on the nape and the squared tail to help identify the Eurasian Collared-Dove.

Stan's Notes: This non-native bird has spread into Texas, having moved into Florida in the early 1980s after inadvertent introduction to the Bahamas. It has been expanding its range across North America and is predicted to spread just like it did through Europe from Asia. Unknown how this "new" bird will affect populations of the native Mourning Dove. Nearly identical to the Ringed Turtle-Dove, a common pet bird. The dark mark on the back of the neck gave rise to the common name. Look for flashes of white in the tail and dark wing tips when it lands or takes off.

Rock Pigeon
Columba livia

YEAR-ROUND

Size:	13" (33 cm)
Male:	No set color pattern. Shades of gray to white with patches of gleaming, iridescent green and blue. Often has a light rump patch.
Female:	same as male
Juvenile:	same as adults
Nest:	platform; female builds; 3–4 broods per year
Eggs:	1–2; white without markings
Incubation:	18–20 days; female and male incubate
Fledging:	25–26 days; female and male feed the young
Migration:	non-migrator
Food:	seeds
Compare:	The Eurasian Collared-Dove (p. 329) has a black collar on the nape. The Mourning Dove (p. 199) is smaller and light brown and lacks the variety of color combinations of the Rock Pigeon.

Stan's Notes: Also known as the Domestic Pigeon. Formerly known as the Rock Dove. Introduced to North America from Europe by the early settlers. Most common around cities and barnyards, where it scratches for seeds. One of the few birds with a wide variety of colors, produced by years of selective breeding while in captivity. Parents feed the young a regurgitated liquid known as crop-milk for the first few days of life. One of the few birds that can drink without tilting its head back. Nests under bridges or on buildings, balconies, barns and sheds. Was once thought to be a nuisance in cities and was poisoned. Now, many cities have Peregrine Falcons (p. 337) feeding on Rock Pigeons, which keeps their numbers in check.

breeding
p. 211

displaying

winter

Willet

Catoptrophorus semipalmatus

YEAR-ROUND
MIGRATION

Size: 14–16" (36–40 cm)

Male: Winter plumage is gray with a white belly. A distinctive black-and-white wing lining pattern, seen in flight or during display. Gray bill and legs.

Female: same as male

Juvenile: similar to breeding adult, more tan in color

Nest: ground; female builds; 1 brood per year

Eggs: 3–5; olive-green with dark markings

Incubation: 24–28 days; male and female incubate

Fledging: 1–2 days; female and male feed young

Migration: complete, to coastal Texas, Mexico, Central America and South America; year-round resident on the Gulf Coast

Food: insects, small fish, crabs, worms, clams

Compare: Greater Yellowlegs (p. 205) is slightly smaller and has a longer neck and yellow legs. Greater Yellowlegs lacks the Willet's distinctive black-and-white wing linings.

Stan's Notes: Seen during migration throughout Texas and a year-round resident along the coast. Northern birds pass through coastal Texas to destinations farther south. It appears a rich, warm brown during the breeding season and rather plain gray during the winter, but it always has a striking black-and-white wing pattern when seen in flight. Uses its black-and-white wing patches to display to its mate. Named after the "pill-will-willet" call it gives during the breeding season. Gives a "kip-kip-kip" alarm call when it takes flight. Nests along the Gulf and East Coasts, in some western states and Canada.

soaring

juvenile

Cooper's Hawk
Accipiter cooperii

YEAR-ROUND
WINTER

Size:	14–20" (36–51 cm); up to 3' wingspan
Male:	Medium-size hawk with short wings and a long, rounded tail with several black bands. Slate-gray back, rusty breast, dark wing tips. Gray bill with a bright-yellow spot at the base. Dark-red eyes.
Female:	similar to male but larger
Juvenile:	brown back, brown streaking on the breast, bright-yellow eyes
Nest:	platform; male and female construct; 1 brood per year
Eggs:	2–4; greenish with brown markings
Incubation:	32–36 days; female and male incubate
Fledging:	28–32 days; male and female feed the young
Migration:	non-migrator to partial migrator; moves around to find food
Food:	small birds, mammals
Compare:	Sharp-shinned Hawk (p. 325) is much smaller, lighter gray and has a squared tail. Red-shouldered Hawk (p. 221) is larger-bodied with a shorter tail. Look for the banded, rounded tail to help identify Cooper's Hawk.

Stan's Notes: Found in many habitats, from woodlands to parks and backyards. Stubby wings help it to navigate around trees while it chases small birds. Will ambush prey, flying into heavy brush or even running on the ground. Comes to feeders, hunting for birds. Flies with long glides followed by a few quick flaps. Calls a loud, clear "cack-cack-cack-cack." The young have gray eyes that turn bright yellow at 1 year and turn dark red later, after 3–5 years.

juvenile

in-flight
juvenile

in flight

Peregrine Falcon
Falco peregrinus

SUMMER
MIGRATION
WINTER

Size: 16–20" (41–51 cm); up to 3¾' wingspan

Male: Dark-gray back and tan-to-white chest. Horizontal bars on belly, legs and undertail. Dark "hood" head marking and wide black mustache. Yellow base of bill and eye-ring. Yellow legs.

Female: similar to male but noticeably larger

Juvenile: overall darker than adults, with heavy streaking on the chest and belly

Nest: ground (scrape) on a cliff edge, tall building, bridge or smokestack; 1 brood per year

Eggs: 3–4; white, some with brown markings

Incubation: 29–32 days; female and male incubate

Fledging: 35–42 days; male and female feed the young

Migration: complete, to coastal Texas

Food: birds (Rock Pigeons in cities, shorebirds and waterfowl in rural areas)

Compare: The American Kestrel (p. 189) is smaller and has 2 vertical black stripes on its face. Look for the dark "hood" head marking and mustache marks to identify the Peregrine Falcon.

Stan's Notes: A wide-bodied raptor that hunts many bird species. The larger females hunt larger prey. Lives in many cities, diving (stooping) on pigeons at speeds of up to 200 miles (322 km) per hour, which knocks them to the ground. Soars with its wings flat, often riding thermals. During courtship, the male brings food to the female and performs aerial displays. Likes to nest on a high ledge or platform for a good view of its territory. A solitary nester and monogamous.

female
p. 251

male

soaring

Northern Harrier
Circus hudsonius

WINTER

Size: 18–22" (45–56 cm); up to 4' wingspan

Male: Slender, low-flying hawk. Silver-gray with a large white rump patch and white belly. Long tail with faint narrow bands. Black wing tips. Yellow eyes.

Female: dark-brown back, brown streaking on breast and belly, large white rump patch, thin black tail bands, black wing tips, yellow eyes

Juvenile: similar to female, with an orange breast

Nest: ground; female and male construct; 1 brood per year

Eggs: 4–8; bluish white without markings

Incubation: 31–32 days; female incubates

Fledging: 30–35 days; male and female feed the young

Migration: complete, to Texas, Mexico, Central America

Food: mice, snakes, insects, small birds

Compare: Slimmer than the Red-tailed Hawk (p. 253). Cooper's Hawk (p. 335) has a rusty breast. Look for a low-gliding hawk with a large white rump patch to identify the male Harrier.

Stan's Notes: One of the easiest of hawks to identify. Glides just above the ground, following the contours of the land while searching for prey. Holds its wings just above horizontal, tilting back and forth in the wind, similar to Turkey Vultures. Formerly called the Marsh Hawk due to its habit of hunting over marshes. Feeds and nests on the ground. Will also preen and rest on the ground. Unlike other hawks, mainly uses its hearing to find prey, followed by sight. At any age, has a distinctive owl-like face disk.

female
p. 237

male

Gadwall
Mareca strepera

YEAR-ROUND
WINTER

Size: 19" (48 cm)

Male: A plump gray duck with a brown head and a distinctive black rump. White belly. Chestnut-tinged wings. Bright-white wing linings. Small white wing patch, seen when swimming. Gray bill.

Female: similar to female Mallard, a mottled brown with a pronounced color change from dark-brown body to light-brown neck and head, bright-white wing linings, small white wing patch, gray bill with orange sides

Juvenile: similar to female

Nest: ground; female lines the nest with fine grass and down feathers plucked from her chest; 1 brood per year

Eggs: 8–11; white without markings

Incubation: 24–27 days; female incubates

Fledging: 48–56 days; young feed themselves

Migration: complete to non-migrator in Texas

Food: aquatic insects

Compare: Male Gadwall is one of the few gray ducks. Look for its distinctive black rump.

Stan's Notes: A duck of shallow marshes. Consumes mostly plant material, dunking its head in water to feed rather than tipping forward, like other dabbling ducks. Walks well on land; feeds in fields and woodlands. Frequently in pairs with other duck species. Nests within 300 feet (90 m) of water. Establishes pair bond in winter.

341

juvenile

in flight

YEAR-ROUND
SUMMER
MIGRATION

Yellow-crowned Night-Heron
Nyctanassa violacea

Size: 24" (60 cm); up to 3½' wingspan

Male: Stocky gray heron with a black head, white cheek patch and yellow-to-white crown. Thick dark bill. Slender yellow legs. Long, thin white plumes extend from the back of head during breeding season.

Female: same as male

Juvenile: brown with white streaks and a dark bill, green legs

Nest: platform; female and male build; 1 brood per year

Eggs: 4–6; light blue without markings

Incubation: 21–25 days; female and male incubate

Fledging: 21–25 days; female and male feed the young

Migration: complete to non-migrator in Texas

Food: aquatic insects, fish, crustaceans

Compare: One of many heron species in Texas. Great Blue Heron (p. 347) is twice as large, has longer legs and lacks a black chin. The distinctively patterned head makes this heron easy to identify.

Stan's Notes: This heron hunts in the evening and early morning, as the common name implies, but it can also be active during the day. Found from coastal mangroves to interior swamps, often hunting fiddler crabs and crayfish. Not uncommon for it to nest in large heron rookeries. Sometimes will nest by itself or in small colonies. Usually seen alone or in small groups. During breeding season, the crown acquires a yellow hue.

in flight

Canada Goose
Branta canadensis

YEAR-ROUND
WINTER

Size: 25–43" (64–109 cm); up to 5½' wingspan

Male: Large gray goose with a black neck and head. White chin and cheek strap.

Female: same as male

Juvenile: same as adults

Nest: platform, on the ground; female builds; 1 brood per year

Eggs: 5–10; white without markings

Incubation: 25–30 days; female incubates

Fledging: 42–55 days; male and female teach the young to feed

Migration: partial migrator to complete, to Texas

Food: aquatic plants, insects, seeds

Compare: rarely confused with any other bird

Stan's Notes: A winter bird throughout Texas with few year-round residents. Calls a classic "honk-honk-honk," especially in flight. Flocks fly in a large V when traveling long distances. Begins breeding in the third year. Adults mate for many years. If threatened, they will hiss as a warning. Males stand as sentinels at the edge of their group and will bob their heads and become aggressive if approached. Adults molt their primary flight feathers while raising their young, rendering family groups temporarily flightless. Several subspecies occur in the U.S. Generally eastern groups are paler than western. Their size also varies, decreasing northward. The smallest subspecies is in the Arctic.

in flight

Great Blue Heron

Ardea herodias

YEAR-ROUND

Size:	42–48" (107–122 cm); up to 6' wingspan
Male:	Tall and gray. Black eyebrows end in long plumes at the back of the head. Long yellow bill. Long feathers at the base of the neck drop down in a kind of necklace. Long legs.
Female:	same as male
Juvenile:	same as adults, but more brown than gray, with a black crown; lacks plumes
Nest:	platform in a colony; male and female build; 1 brood per year
Eggs:	3–5; blue-green without markings
Incubation:	27–28 days; female and male incubate
Fledging:	56–60 days; male and female feed the young
Migration:	non-migrator in Texas
Food:	small fish, frogs, insects, snakes, baby birds
Compare:	Tricolored Heron (p. 129) is half the size of the Great Blue Heron and has a white belly. The Green Heron (p. 361) is much smaller and has a short neck. The Sandhill Crane (p. 349) has a red cap. Look for the long, yellow bill to help identify the Great Blue Heron.

Stan's Notes: One of the most common herons. Found in open water, from small ponds to large lakes. Stalks small fish in shallow water. Will strike at mice, squirrels and nearly anything it comes across. Red-winged Blackbirds will attack it to stop it from taking their babies out of the nest. In flight, it holds its neck in an S shape and slightly cups its wings, while the legs trail straight out behind. Nests in a colony of up to 100 birds. Nests in trees near or hanging over water. Barks like a dog when startled.

in flight

rusty
stain

in-flight
rusty stain

Sandhill Crane

Grus canadensis

MIGRATION
WINTER

Size: 42–48" (107–122 cm); up to 7' wingspan

Male: Elegant gray crane with long legs and neck. Wings and body often rust brown from mud staining. Scarlet-red cap. Yellow to red eyes.

Female: same as male

Juvenile: dull brown with yellow eyes; lacks a red cap

Nest: ground; female and male construct; 1 brood per year

Eggs: 2; olive with brown markings

Incubation: 28–32 days; female and male incubate

Fledging: 65 days; female and male feed the young

Migration: complete, to Texas and Mexico

Food: insects, fruit, worms, plants, amphibians

Compare: Great Blue Heron (p. 347) has a longer bill and holds its neck in an S shape during flight. The Whooping Crane (p. 409) is taller with white plumage and a red mark behind bill. Look for the scarlet-red cap to help identify the Sandhill Crane.

Stan's Notes: Preens mud into its feathers, staining its plumage rust brown (see insets). Gives a very loud and distinctive rattling call, often heard before the bird is seen. Flight is characteristic, with a faster upstroke, making the wings look like they're flicking in flight. Can fly at heights of over 10,000 feet (3,050 m). Nests on the ground in a large mound of aquatic vegetation. Performs a spectacular mating dance: The birds will face each other, then bow and jump into the air while making loud cackling sounds and flapping their wings. They will also flip sticks and grass into the air during their dance.

male

female

Ruby-throated Hummingbird
Archilochus colubris

YEAR-ROUND
SUMMER

Size: 3–3½" (7.5–9 cm)

Male: Tiny iridescent green bird with black throat patch that reflects bright ruby red in sun.

Female: same as male, but lacking the throat patch

Juvenile: same as female

Nest: cup; female builds; 1–2 broods per year

Eggs: 2; white without markings

Incubation: 12–14 days; female incubates

Fledging: 14–18 days; female feeds the young

Migration: complete, to Mexico and Central America

Food: nectar, insects; will come to nectar feeders

Compare: No other bird is as tiny. The Sphinx Moth also hovers at flowers but has clear wings, doesn't hum in flight, moves much slower than the Ruby-throated and can be approached.

Stan's Notes: This is the smallest bird in the state. Can fly straight up, straight down or backward and hover in midair. Does not sing but chatters or buzzes to communicate. Weighs about the same as a U.S. penny; it takes about five average-sized hummingbirds to equal the weight of one chickadee. The wings create the humming sound. Flaps 50–60 times or more per second when flying at top speed. Breathes 250 times per minute. Heart beats up to 1,260 times per minute. Builds a stretchy nest with plant material and spiderwebs, gluing pieces of lichen to the exterior for camouflage. Attracted to colorful, tubular flowers. Will extract and eat insects trapped in spiderwebs.

male

female

Black-chinned Hummingbird

Archilochus alexandri

SUMMER MIGRATION

Size: 3¾" (9.5 cm)

Male: Tiny iridescent green bird with black throat patch (gorget) that reflects violet-blue in sunlight. Black chin. White chest and belly.

Female: same as male, but lacking the throat patch and black chin, has white flanks

Juvenile: similar to female

Nest: cup; female builds; 1–2 broods per year

Eggs: 1–3; white without markings

Incubation: 13–16 days; female incubates

Fledging: 19–21 days; female feeds young

Migration: complete, to Central and South America

Food: nectar, insects; will come to nectar feeders

Compare: The male Ruby-throated (p. 351) is similar, but it has a ruby-red throat patch. Look for the violet-blue throat patch and what often appears to be an all-black head to help identify the Male Black-chinned.

Stan's Notes: One of several hummingbird species in Texas. Can fly backward, but doesn't sing. Will chatter or buzz to communicate. Wings create a humming noise, flapping nearly 80 times per second. Weighing only 2–3 grams, it takes approximately five average-sized hummingbirds to equal the weight of one chickadee. Males return first at the end of April. Male performs a spectacular pendulum-like flight over a perched female. After mating, the female builds a nest, using spiderwebs to glue nest materials together, and raises young without the mate's help. More than one clutch per year not uncommon.

male

female

Painted Bunting
Passerina ciris

SUMMER

Size: 5½" (14 cm)

Male: An amazing combination of colors. A green back, deep-blue head and orange chest and belly. Dark wings and tail.

Female: bright green above, light green below

Juvenile: drab version of the female with only some small spots of green

Nest: cup; female and male construct; 1–2 broods per year

Eggs: 3–5; pale blue with brown markings

Incubation: 11–12 days; female incubates

Fledging: 12–14 days; female and male feed the young

Migration: complete, to Mexico and Central America

Food: seeds, insects; will visit seed feeders

Compare: No other bird can compare with the male's striking colors. The female is uniquely green and rarely confused with any other bird.

Stan's Notes: A wonderful bunting of backyard gardens, woodland edges and along brushy roads. Visits seed feeders in wooded yards. Well known for its loud, clear and varied warbling phrases. Cup nest, made of grass and lined with animal hair, is usually in a deep, tangled mass of vines. A common cowbird host, this unfortunately often results in it raising the cowbird young and not its own. Nests across most of Texas. Often captured in Central America and sold as a caged bird; both activities are illegal in the U.S. and should not be supported.

Green-tailed Towhee
Pipilo chlorurus

MIGRATION
WINTER

Size: 7¼" (18.5 cm)

Male: A unique yellowish-green back, wings and tail. Dark-gray chest and face. Bright-white throat with black stripes. Rusty-red crown.

Female: same as male

Juvenile: olive-green with heavy streaking on breast and belly, lacks crown and throat markings of adult

Nest: cup; female and male construct; 1–2 broods per year

Eggs: 3–5; white with brown markings

Incubation: 12–14 days; female and male incubate

Fledging: 10–14 days; female and male feed young

Migration: complete, to parts of Texas and to Mexico

Food: insects, seeds, fruit

Compare: Green Jay (p. 359) is larger and has a blue crown and black throat. Green-tailed's unusual color, short wings, long tail and large bill make it easy to identify.

Stan's Notes: Seen during migration and in winter in some parts of Texas. Found on shrubby hillsides and sagebrush mountain slopes up to 7,000 feet (2,150 m). Like other towhees, searches for insects and seeds, taking a little jump forward while kicking backward with both feet. Known to scurry away from trouble, jumping to ground without opening its wings and running across the ground.

Green Jay
Cyanocorax yncas

YEAR-ROUND

Size: 10½" (27 cm)

Male: A uniquely colored and patterned bird. Pale-green body and wings. Blue crown and face. Black chin, throat and upper breast. Yellow belly, wings, outer tail feathers and underside of tail.

Female: same as male

Juvenile: similar to adult, but not as brightly colored

Nest: cup; female and male construct; 1 brood per year

Eggs: 3–5; pale white to gray with brown marks

Incubation: 17–18 days; female and male incubate

Fledging: 18–22 days; female and male feed young

Migration: non-migrator; moves around to find food

Food: seeds, fruit, nectar, nuts, carrion, small mammals; comes to seed and fruit feeders

Compare: A unique bird with a combination of green, blue and yellow.

Stan's Notes: Tropical bird restricted to southern Texas in the U.S., but range extends to Central America. Also known as Rio Grande Jay. Travels in noisy family groups of up to ten or more. Found mainly in dense vegetation, with a small home territory. A strong flier, often gliding between perches or to ground. Flashes bright yellow under wings in flight. An inquisitive, friendly bird, quickly investigating feeders or fruit. Caches food, burying acorns. Steals acorns from other birds. Only one pair breeds in a flock. Like other jays it has helpers, usually family members, to help raise the young. Two-year-old birds are dispersed from the family unit by parents.

in flight

Green Heron
Butorides virescens

YEAR-ROUND
SUMMER

Size: 16–22" (41–56 cm)

Male: Short and stocky. Blue-green back and rust-red neck and breast. Dark-green crest. Short legs are normally yellow but turn bright orange during the breeding season.

Female: same as male

Juvenile: similar to adults, with a bluish-gray back and white-streaked breast and neck

Nest: platform; female and male build; 2 broods per year

Eggs: 2–4; light green without markings

Incubation: 21–25 days; female and male incubate

Fledging: 35–36 days; female and male feed the young

Migration: complete to non-migrator, to coastal Texas, Mexico, Central America and South America

Food: small fish, aquatic insects, small amphibians

Compare: Tricolored Heron (p. 129) is smaller. Great Blue Heron (p. 347) is larger. Green Heron lacks the long neck of other herons. Look for a small heron with a dark-green back and crest to identify the Green.

Stan's Notes: Often gives an explosive, rasping "skyew" call when startled. Holds its head close to its body, which sometimes makes it look like it doesn't have a neck. Waits on the shore or wades stealthily, hunting for small fish, aquatic insects and small amphibians. Places an object, such as an insect, on the water's surface to attract fish to catch. Nests in a tall tree, often a short distance from the water. The nest can be very high up in the tree. Babies give a loud ticking sound, like the ticktock of a clock.

female
p. 233

male

Wood Duck
Aix sponsa

YEAR-ROUND
SUMMER
WINTER

Size: 17–20" (43–51 cm)

Male: Small, highly ornamented dabbling duck. Mostly green head and crest patterned with black and white. Rusty chest and a white belly. Red eyes.

Female: brown duck with a bright-white eye-ring, not-so-obvious crest and blue patch on wings (speculum), often hidden

Juvenile: similar to female

Nest: cavity; female lines an old woodpecker cavity or a nest box in a tree; 1 brood per year

Eggs: 10–15; creamy white without markings

Incubation: 28–36 days; female incubates

Fledging: 56–68 days; female teaches the young to feed

Migration: non-migrator to partial migrator in Texas

Food: aquatic insects, plants, seeds

Compare: Male Northern Shoveler (p. 367) is larger with a long wide bill. Similar in size to male Hooded Merganser (p. 87), which has a crest "hood" it raises to reveal a large white patch.

Stan's Notes: A duck of quiet, shallow backwater ponds. Nearly extinct around 1900 due to overhunting, doing well now. Nests in tree cavity or nest box. Seen flying in forests or perching on high branches. Female takes off with a loud squealing call and enters the nest cavity from full flight. Lays some eggs in a neighboring nest (egg dumping), resulting in more than 20 eggs in some clutches. Hatchlings stay in nest for 24 hours, then jump from as high as 60 feet (18 m) to the ground or water to follow their mother. They never return to the nest.

female
p. 243

male

Mallard
Anas platyrhynchos

YEAR-ROUND
WINTER

Size: 19–21" (48–53 cm)

Male: Large, bulbous green head, white necklace and rust-brown or chestnut chest. Gray-and-white sides. Yellow bill. Orange legs and feet.

Female: brown with an orange-and-black bill and blue-and-white wing mark (speculum)

Juvenile: same as female but with a yellow bill

Nest: ground; female builds; 1 brood per year

Eggs: 7–10; greenish to whitish, unmarked

Incubation: 26–30 days; female incubates

Fledging: 42–52 days; female leads the young to food

Migration: non-migrator in Texas, joined by birds from further north in winter

Food: seeds, plants, aquatic insects; will come to ground feeders offering corn

Compare: Male Northern Shoveler (p. 367) has a white chest with rusty sides and a very large, spoon-shaped bill. Breeding male Northern Pintail (p. 245) has long tail feathers and a brown head. Look for the green head and yellow bill to identify the male Mallard.

Stan's Notes: A familiar dabbling duck of lakes and ponds. Also found in rivers, streams and some backyards. Tips forward to feed on vegetation on the bottom of shallow water. The name "Mallard" comes from the Latin word *masculus*, meaning "male," referring to the male's habit of taking no part in raising the young. Male and female have white underwings and white tails, but only the male has black central tail feathers that curl upward. Unlike the female, the male doesn't quack. Returns to its birthplace each year.

female
p. 241

male

Northern Shoveler
Anas clypeata

WINTER

Size: 19–21" (48–53 cm)

Male: Medium-sized duck with an iridescent green head, rust sides, white chest. Extraordinarily large, spoon-shaped bill, almost always held pointed toward the water.

Female: brown and black all over, green wing patch (speculum) and a large spoon-shaped bill

Juvenile: same as female

Nest: ground; female builds; 1 brood per year

Eggs: 9–12; olive without markings

Incubation: 22–25 days; female incubates

Fledging: 30–60 days; female leads the young to food

Migration: complete, to Texas, Mexico, Central America

Food: aquatic insects, plants

Compare: Male Mallard (p. 365) is similar, but it lacks the large spoon-shaped bill. The male Wood Duck (p. 363) is smaller and has a crest.

Stan's Notes: One of several species of shovelers. Called "Shoveler" due to the peculiar, shovel-like shape of its bill. Given the common name "Northern" because it is the only species of these ducks in North America. Seen in shallow wetlands, ponds and small lakes in flocks of 5–10 birds. Flocks fly in tight formation. Swims low in water, pointing its large bill toward the water as if it's too heavy to lift. Usually swims in tight circles while feeding. Feeds mainly by filtering tiny aquatic insects and plants from the surface of the water with its bill. Female gathers plant material and forms it into a nest a short distance from the water. Winters in Texas where it can find water.

male

female

Rufous Hummingbird
Selasphorus rufus

Size: 3¾" (9.5 cm)

Male: Tiny burnt-orange bird with a black throat patch (gorget) that reflects orange-red in sunlight. White chest. Green-to-tan flanks.

Female: same as male, but lacking the throat patch

Juvenile: similar to female

Nest: cup; female builds; 1–2 broods per year

Eggs: 1–3; white without markings

Incubation: 14–17 days; female incubates

Fledging: 21–26 days; female feeds young

Migration: complete, to Texas and Mexico

Food: nectar, insects; will come to nectar feeders

Compare: Ruby-throated Hummingbird (p. 351) is slightly smaller and more common. Identify it by the unique orange-red (rufous) color.

Stan's Notes: One of the smallest birds in the state. This is a bold, hardy hummer. Frequently seen well out of its normal range in the western U.S., showing up along the East Coast. Visits hummingbird feeders in your yard during migration. Does not sing, but it will chatter or buzz to communicate. Weighing just 2–3 grams, it takes about five average-sized hummingbirds to equal the weight of one chickadee. The heart beats up to an incredible 1,260 times per minute. Male performs a spectacular pendulum-like flight over the perched female. After mating, the female will fly off to build a nest and raise young, without any help from her mate. Constructs a soft, flexible nest that expands to accommodate the growing young.

female
p. 427

male

Baltimore Oriole

Icterus galbula

Size: 7–8" (18–20 cm)

Male: Flaming orange with a black head and back. White-and-orange wing bars. Orange-and-black tail. Gray bill and dark eyes.

Female: pale yellow with orange tones, gray-brown wings, white wing bars, gray bill, dark eyes

Juvenile: same as female

Nest: pendulous; female builds; 1 brood per year

Eggs: 4–5; bluish with brown markings

Incubation: 12–14 days; female incubates

Fledging: 12–14 days; female and male feed the young

Migration: complete, to Mexico, Central America and South America

Food: insects, fruit, nectar; comes to nectar, orange-half and grape-jelly feeders

Compare: The male Bullock's Oriole (p. 375) lacks the black "hood." The male Orchard Oriole (p. 373) is much darker orange. Look for the flaming orange to identify the male Baltimore Oriole.

Stan's Notes: A fantastic songster, often heard before seen. Easily attracted to a feeder that offers sugar water (nectar), orange halves or grape jelly. Parents bring their young to feeders. Sits at the top of trees, feeding on caterpillars. Female builds a sock-like nest at the outermost branches of tall trees. Prefers parks, yards and forests and often returns to the same area year after year. Young males turn orange-and-black at 1½ years of age. Some of the last birds to arrive in spring (April to May) and first to leave in fall (September).

female
p. 429

male

first-year
male

Orchard Oriole
Icterus spurius

SUMMER

Size: 7–8" (18–20 cm)

Male: Dark orange with black head, throat, upper back, wings and tail. White wing bar. Bill is long and thin. Gray mark on lower bill.

Female: olive-green back, dull-yellow belly and gray wings with 2 indistinct white wing bars

Juvenile: same as female; first-year male looks like the female, with a black bib

Nest: pendulous; female builds; 1 brood per year

Eggs: 3–5; pale blue to white, brown markings

Incubation: 11–12 days; female and male incubate

Fledging: 11–14 days; female and male feed the young

Migration: complete, to Mexico, Central America and northern South America

Food: insects, fruit, nectar; comes to nectar, orange-half and grape-jelly feeders

Compare: The male Baltimore Oriole (p. 371) is brighter orange. Look for the dark-orange plumage to identify the male Orchard Oriole.

Stan's Notes: Named "Orchard" for its preference for orchards. Also likes open woods. Eats insects until wild fruit starts to ripen. Often nests alone; sometimes nests in small colonies. Parents bring their young to bird feeding stations after they fledge. Many people don't see these birds at their feeders very much during the summer and think they have left, but the birds are still there, hunting for insects to feed to their young. One of the last birds to arrive in spring and one of the first to leave in fall. Spends 4–5 months in Texas. Often migrates in flocks with Baltimore Orioles.

female
p. 431

male

Bullock's Oriole

Icterus bullockii

SUMMER

Size: 8" (20 cm)

Male: Bright-orange-and-black bird. Black crown, eye line, nape, chin, back and wings with a bold white patch on wings.

Female: dull yellow overall, pale-white belly, white wing bars on gray-to-black wings

Juvenile: similar to female

Nest: pendulous; female and male build; 1 brood per year

Eggs: 4–6; pale white to gray, brown markings

Incubation: 12–14 days; female incubates

Fledging: 12–14 days; female and male feed young

Migration: complete, to Mexico and Central America

Food: insects, berries, nectar; visits nectar feeders

Compare: Male Baltimore Oriole (p. 371) has a black hood. Look for Bullock's bright markings and a thin black line running through each eye.

Stan's Notes: So closely related to Baltimore Orioles of the eastern U.S., at one time both were considered a single species. Interbreeds with Baltimores where their ranges overlap. Most common in the state where cottonwood trees grow along rivers and other wetlands. Also found at edges of clearings, in city parks, on farms and along irrigation ditches. Hanging sock-like nest is constructed of plant fibers such as inner bark of junipers and willows. Will incorporate yarn and thread into its nest if offered at the time of nest building.

female
p. 171

male

Black-headed Grosbeak
Pheucticus melanocephalus

SUMMER MIGRATION

Size: 8" (20 cm)

Male: Stocky bird with burnt-orange chest, neck and rump. Black head, tail and wings. Irregularly shaped white wing patches. Large bill, with upper bill darker than lower.

Female: appears like an overgrown sparrow, overall brown with a lighter breast and belly, large two-toned bill, prominent white eyebrows, yellow wing linings, as seen in flight

Juvenile: similar to adult of the same sex

Nest: cup; female builds; 1 brood per year

Eggs: 3–4; pale green or bluish, brown markings

Incubation: 11–13 days; female and male incubate

Fledging: 11–13 days; female and male feed young

Migration: complete, to Mexico

Food: seeds, insects, fruit; comes to seed feeders

Compare: The male Bullock's Oriole (p. 375) has more white on wings than the male Black-headed. Look for Black-headed's large bicolored bill.

Stan's Notes: A cosmopolitan bird that nests in a wide variety of habitats. Both the male and female sing and will aggressively defend the nest against intruders. Song is very similar to American Robin's, making it hard to tell them apart by song. Populations increasing in Texas and across the U.S.

male

female
p. 137

yellow
male

House Finch
Haemorhous mexicanus

YEAR-ROUND

Size: 5" (13 cm)

Male: Small finch with a red-to-orange face, throat, chest and rump. Brown cap. Brown marking behind eyes. White belly with brown streaks. Brown wings with white streaks.

Female: brown with a heavily streaked white chest

Juvenile: similar to female

Nest: cup, sometimes in cavities; female builds; 2 broods per year

Eggs: 4–5; pale blue, lightly marked

Incubation: 12–14 days; female incubates

Fledging: 15–19 days; female and male feed the young

Migration: non-migrator; moves around to find food

Food: seeds, fruit, leaf buds; visits seed feeders and feeders that offer grape jelly

Compare: The male Vermilion Flycatcher (p. 381) has a black nape, back and wings. Look for the brown cap and streaked belly to help identify the male House Finch.

Stan's Notes: Can be a common bird at your feeders. Very social, visiting feeders in small flocks. Likes to nest in hanging flower baskets. Male sings a loud, cheerful warbling song. It was originally introduced to Long Island, New York, from the western U.S. in the 1940s and is now found throughout the country. Suffers from a disease that causes the eyes to crust, resulting in blindness and death. Rarely, males are yellow (inset), perhaps due to poor diet.

female
p. 295

male

Vermilion Flycatcher
Pyrocephalus rubinus

SUMMER
WINTER

Size: 6" (15 cm)

Male: A stunningly beautiful bird with a crimson-red head, crest, chin, breast and belly. Black nape, back, wings and tail. Thick black line running through eyes. Thin black bill.

Female: gray head, neck and back, nearly white chin and breast, pink belly to undertail, black tail, thin black bill

Juvenile: similar to female, lacks a pink undertail

Nest: cup; female builds; 1–2 broods per year

Eggs: 2–4; white with brown markings

Incubation: 14–16 days; female and male incubate

Fledging: 14–16 days; female and male feed young

Migration: complete; to Mexico

Food: insects (mainly bees)

Compare: The unique bright crimson plumage with black wings make this bird easy to identify.

Stan's Notes: A uniquely colored flycatcher with few staying all winter in extreme southern Texas. Often found in open areas with shrubs and small trees close to water. Feeds mainly on insects, with bees making up a large part of its diet. Will perch on a thin branch, pumping tail up and down while waiting for an aerial insect. Flies out to snatch it, then returns to the perch. Drops to the ground for terrestrial insects. Male raises its crest, fluffs chest feathers, fans tail and sings a song during a fluttery flight to court females. Female builds a shallow nest of twigs and grasses and lines it with downy plant material. Male feeds female during incubation and brooding.

female
p. 433

male

Summer Tanager
Piranga rubra

SUMMER

Size: 8" (20 cm)

Male: Bright rosy-red bird with darker red wings.

Female: overall yellow with slightly darker wings

Juvenile: male has patches of red and green over the entire body, female is same as adult female

Nest: cup; female builds; 1–2 broods per year

Eggs: 3–5; pale blue with dark markings

Incubation: 10–12 days; female incubates

Fledging: 12–15 days; female and male feed young

Migration: complete, to Central and South America

Food: insects, fruit

Compare: Similar size as the male Northern Cardinal (p. 385), but the male Cardinal has a black mask, large crest and red bill.

Stan's Notes: Found in Texas where woodlands exist, especially in mixed pine and oak forests. Due to clearing of land for agriculture, populations have decreased for over a century and especially most recently. Returning to Texas in late April and with young hatching in late May, some pairs have two broods per year. While fruit makes up some of the diet, most of it consists of insects such as bees and wasps. Summer Tanagers unfortunately seem to be parasitized by Brown-headed Cowbirds.

female
p. 177

male

juvenile

Northern Cardinal
Cardinalis cardinalis

YEAR-ROUND

Size: 8–9" (20–23 cm)

Male: Red with a black mask that extends from the face to the throat. Large crest and a large red bill.

Female: buff-brown with a black mask, large reddish bill, and red tinges on the crest and wings

Juvenile: same as female but with a blackish-gray bill

Nest: cup; female builds; 2–3 broods per year

Eggs: 3–4; bluish white with brown markings

Incubation: 12–13 days; female and male incubate

Fledging: 9–10 days; female and male feed the young

Migration: non-migrator

Food: seeds, insects, fruit; comes to seed feeders

Compare: Similar size as the male Summer Tanager (p. 383), but the male Tanager is rosy red. Look for the black mask, large crest and red bill to identify the male Northern Cardinal.

Stan's Notes: A familiar backyard bird. Seen in a variety of habitats, including parks. Usually likes thick vegetation. One of the few species in which both males and females sing. Can be heard all year. Listen for its "whata-cheer-cheer-cheer" territorial call in spring. Watch for a male feeding a female during courtship. The male also feeds the young of the first brood while the female builds a second nest. Territorial in spring, fighting its own reflection in a window or other reflective surface. Non-territorial in winter, gathering in small flocks of up to 20 birds. Makes short flights from cover to cover, often landing on the ground. *Cardinalis* denotes importance, as represented by the red priestly garments of Catholic cardinals.

female p. 239

male

Redhead

Aythya americana

Size: 19" (48 cm)

Male: Rich-red head and neck with a black breast and tail, gray sides, and smoky-gray wings and back. Tricolored bill with a light-blue base, white ring and black tip.

Female: soft-brown, plain-looking duck with gray to white wing linings, a rounded top of head and a gray bill with a black tip

Juvenile: similar to female

Nest: cup; female builds; 1 brood per year

Eggs: 9–14; white without markings

Incubation: 24–28 days; female and male incubate

Fledging: 56–73 days; female shows young what to eat

Migration: complete, to Texas

Food: seeds, aquatic plants, insects

Compare: The male Northern Shoveler (p. 367) has a green head and rusty sides, unlike the red head and gray sides of the male Redhead.

Stan's Notes: A duck of permanent large bodies of water. Forages along the shoreline, feeding on seeds, aquatic plants and insects. Usually builds nest directly on the water's surface, using large mats of vegetation. Female lays up to 75 percent of its eggs in the nests of other Redheads and several other duck species. Nests primarily in the Prairie Pothole region of the northern Great Plains. The overall populations seem to be increasing at about 2–3 percent each year. Winters throughout Texas where it can find water.

male

Canvasback
Aythya valisineria

WINTER

Size: 20–21" (51–53 cm)

Male: Deep-red head with a sloping forehead that transitions into a long black bill. Red neck. Gray-and-white sides and back. Black chest and tail.

Female: similar to male, but has a brown head, neck and chest, light gray-to-brown sides and a long dark bill

Juvenile: similar to female

Nest: ground; female builds; 1 brood per year

Eggs: 7–9; pale white to gray without markings

Incubation: 24–29 days; female incubates

Fledging: 56–67 days; female leads young to food

Migration: complete, to Texas and Mexico

Food: aquatic insects, small clams

Compare: The male Lesser Scaup (p. 85) is smaller, lacks the red head and neck of the male Canvasback and has a shorter, light blue bill.

Stan's Notes: A large inland duck of freshwater lakes, rivers and ponds. Populations declined dramatically in the 1960–80s due to marsh drainage for agriculture. Females return to their birthplace (philopatric) while males disperse to new areas. Will mate during migration or on the breeding grounds. A courting male gives a soft cooing call when displaying and during aerial chases. Male leaves the female after incubation starts. Female takes a new mate every year. Female feeds very little during incubation and will lose up to 70 percent of fat reserves during that time.

in flight

juvenile

Roseate Spoonbill

Platalea ajaja

YEAR-ROUND
SUMMER

Size: 30–34" (80 cm); up to 4' wingspan

Male: An overall pink bird with red highlights. White neck with a black patch on the back of the head. Heavy, spoon-shaped flat bill. Long red legs.

Female: same as male

Juvenile: pale version of adult

Nest: platform; female and male build; 1 brood per year

Eggs: 1–4; olive green with dark markings

Incubation: 22–23 days; male and female incubate

Fledging: 35–42 days; female and male feed young

Migration: partial migrator to non-migrator

Food: fish, aquatic insects, snails, worms, leeches

Compare: This is an unmistakable bird of Texas. The Roseate Spoonbill is larger than White Ibis (p. 403) and has a long, down-curved orange-to-red bill, unlike the heavy flat bill of the Spoonbill.

Stan's Notes: A summer resident in eastern parts of Texas and a year-round Gulf Coast resident. This bird is making a comeback from devastating hunting pressures in the 1800s for its wing feathers, which were used in women's hats and fans. Now habitat destruction is limiting its numbers. Swings its spoon-shaped bill to sift fish and insects from shallow waters. Usually seen in small flocks. Nests in mixed colonies with herons. Related to the ibises.

in flight

breeding

in flight

winter

Laughing Gull
Leucophaeus atricilla

YEAR-ROUND

Size: 16–17" (40–43 cm); up to 3⅓' wingspan

Male: Breeding adult has a black head "hood" and white neck, chest and belly. Slate-gray back and wings with black wing tips. Orange bill. Incomplete white eye-ring. Winter plumage lacks the "hood" and has a black bill.

Female: same as male

Juvenile: brown throughout, gray sides, lacking the black head and white chest, has a gray bill

Nest: ground; male and female construct; 1 brood per year

Eggs: 2–4; olive with brown markings

Incubation: 18–20 days; female and male incubate

Fledging: 30–35 days; male and female feed young

Migration: non-migrator along coastal Texas

Food: fish, insects, aquatic insects

Compare: Ring-billed Gull (p. 395) is larger. Look for the black head "hood" and slate-gray back and wings of the Laughing Gull.

Stan's Notes: This is a three-year gull that starts out mostly brown and gray. The second year it resembles adults but lacks a complete black head "hood." Breeding plumage in the third year. Male tosses its head back and calls to attract a mate. Nests in marshes in large colonies. Nest is a scrape on the ground lined with grass, sticks and rocks. Adults feed young half-digested food. Name comes from its laugh-like call.

in flight

breeding

juvenile

winter

Ring-billed Gull

Larus delawarensis

YEAR-ROUND
WINTER

Size: 18–20" (45–51 cm); up to 4' wingspan

Male: White with gray wings, black wing tips spotted with white, and a white tail, seen in flight (inset). Yellow bill with a black ring near the tip. Yellowish legs and feet. In winter, the back of the head and the nape of the neck are speckled brown.

Female: same as male

Juvenile: white with brown speckles and a brown tip of tail; mostly dark bill

Nest: ground; female and male construct; 1 brood per year

Eggs: 2–4; off-white with brown markings

Incubation: 20–21 days; female and male incubate

Fledging: 20–40 days; female and male feed the young

Migration: complete to non-migrator in Texas

Food: insects, fish; scavenges for food

Compare: Laughing Gull (p. 393) has a black head "hood." Look for a large white gull with a black ring around the bill near the tip.

Stan's Notes: A common gull of garbage dumps and parking lots. One of the most common gulls in the U.S. Hundreds of these birds often flock together. A three-year gull with different plumages in each of its first three years. Attains the ring on its bill after the first winter and adult plumage in the third year. Defends a small area around the nest, usually only a few feet.

in flight

Cattle Egret
Bubulcus ibis

YEAR-ROUND
SUMMER

Size: 18–22" (45–56 cm); up to 3' wingspan

Male: White with orange-buff crest, breast and back. Stocky with a disproportionally large round head. Red-orange bill and legs. Winter plumage is all white with a yellow bill and dark legs.

Female: same as male

Juvenile: similar to winter adult but with a dark bill

Nest: platform; female and male build; 1 brood per year

Eggs: 2–5; light blue-green without markings

Incubation: 22–26 days; female and male incubate

Fledging: 28–30 days; female and male feed the young

Migration: partial to non-migrator in Texas; will move around to find food

Food: insects, small mammals

Compare: Great Egret (p. 407) is about twice as large and has a much longer neck and a much larger bill. White Ibis (p. 403) has a large down-curved bill.

Stan's Notes: Came to South America from Africa around 1880, reaching Florida in the 1940s. Started being seen in Texas in the mid-1950s. Often seen solo in pastures, hunting insects at cow and horse pies by wiggling its neck and head back and forth and from side to side, while holding its body still. Then it stabs at prey and tosses it to the back of its mouth. Frequently attracted to field fires to hunt newly exposed animals and insects. In some years it is found as far as northern-tier states and Canada.

winter

in flight

breeding

Caspian Tern
Sterna caspia

YEAR-ROUND
MIGRATION

Size: 21" (53 cm); up to 4' wingspan

Male: White chest and belly. Light-gray back. White wing surfaces below and light gray above, with black tips, as seen in flight. Black cap extends over eyes. Large dark-red bill with darker tip. Black legs. Winter plumage has a streaked cap.

Female: same as male

Juvenile: similar to winter adult, orange bill

Nest: ground; female and male construct; 1 brood per year

Eggs: 1–4; pinkish with brown markings

Incubation: 20–22 days; female and male incubate

Fledging: 30–40 days; female and male feed the young

Migration: non-migrator along coastal Texas

Food: fish, aquatic insects

Compare: Smaller and more streamlined than most gulls, with thinner wings than gull wings. Look for the large red bill and black cap.

Stan's Notes: A large strong tern with a deep, harsh loud scream. Frequently seen in large groups flying at about 30 feet (9 m) above water, patrolling for fish. Nests in large colonies on small islands and sand beaches. The young recognize the calls of their parents, which help them find each other when adults return to the colony with food. Young chase adults until they are fed. Adults feed young for up to seven months, the longest time of any tern species.

in flight

Snowy Egret
Egretta thula

YEAR-ROUND
SUMMER
MIGRATION

Size: 22–26" (56–66 cm); up to 3½' wingspan

Male: All-white bird with black bill. Black legs. Bright-yellow feet. Long feather plumes on head, neck and back during breeding season.

Female: same as male

Juvenile: similar to adult, but backs of legs are yellow

Nest: platform; female and male build; 1 brood per year

Eggs: 3–5; light blue-green without markings

Incubation: 20–24 days; female and male incubate

Fledging: 28–30 days; female and male feed the young

Migration: partial migrator to non-migrator in Texas

Food: aquatic insects, small fish

Compare: Great Egret (p. 407) is much larger and has a yellow bill and black feet. Juvenile Little Blue Heron (p. 127) is the same size and has a black-tipped gray bill. Look for the black bill and yellow feet of Snowy Egret to help identify.

Stan's Notes: Common in wetlands and often seen with other egrets. Colonies may include up to several hundred nests. Nests are low in shrubs 5–10 feet (1.5–3 m) tall or constructs a nest on the ground, usually mixed among other egret and heron nests. Chicks hatch days apart (asynchronous), leading to starvation of last to hatch. Will actively "hunt" prey by moving around quickly, stirring up small fish and aquatic insects with its feet. In the breeding state, a yellow patch at the base of bill and the yellow feet turn orange-red. Was hunted to near extinction in the late 1800s for its feathers.

in flight

juvenile

White Ibis
Eudocimus albus

YEAR-ROUND

Size:	23–27" (58–69 cm); up to 3' wingspan
Male:	All-white bird with a very long, downward-curving orange-to-red bill. Pink facial skin. Color of legs matches the bill color. Black wing tips, seen only in flight.
Female:	same as male, but smaller; downward curve of bill is less than curve of male bill
Juvenile:	combination of chocolate-brown and white for the first two years, dull-orange bill
Nest:	platform; female and male build; 1 brood per year
Eggs:	2–3; light blue with dark markings
Incubation:	21–23 days; female and male incubate
Fledging:	28–35 days; female and male feed the young
Migration:	non-migrator along coastal Texas
Food:	aquatic insects, crustaceans, fish
Compare:	One of two ibis species in Texas. White-faced Ibis (p. 267) is brown and slightly smaller. Snowy Egret (p. 401) has a straight black bill and bright-yellow feet. Look for the long down- curved bill to help identify the White Ibis.

Stan's Notes: Has been increasing in Texas over the past 50 years, with inland sightings getting more common. A year-round resident along the coast. Prefers fresh water over salt water, with crayfish a big part of its diet. White plumage with black wing tips and a bright orange-to-red down-curved bill make this species easy to identify. Frequently seen flying in groups of 30 or more. Nests in large colonies in well-made stick nests.

white
morph

blue morph

juvenile

Ross's Goose

in flight

Snow Goose
Chen caerulescens

MIGRATION
WINTER

Size: 25–38" (64–97 cm); up to 4½' wingspan

Male: White morph has black wing tips and varying patches of black and brown. Blue morph has a white head and a gray breast and back. Both morphs have a pink bill and legs.

Female: same as male

Juvenile: overall dull gray with a dark bill

Nest: ground; female builds; 1 brood per year

Eggs: 3–5; white without markings

Incubation: 23–25 days; female incubates

Fledging: 45–49 days; female and male teach the young to feed

Migration: complete, to coastal Texas, Mexico

Food: aquatic insects and plants

Compare: The Canada Goose (p. 345) is larger and has a black neck and white chin strap. The American White Pelican (p. 411) shares black wing tips, but it has an enormous bill.

Stan's Notes: This bird occurs in light (white) and dark (blue) color morphs. The white morph is more common than the blue. A bird of wide-open fields, wetlands and lakes of any size. It has a thick, serrated bill, which helps it to grab and pull up plants. Breeds in large colonies on the northern tundra in Canada. Female starts to breed at 2–3 years. Older females produce more eggs and are more successful at reproduction than younger females. Seen by the thousands during migration and in winter. Very similar to the Ross's Goose (see inset), which is slightly smaller and has a much smaller pink bill. Commonly seen with Ross's Geese and Sandhill Cranes. Has a classic goose-like call.

in flight

Great Egret
Ardea alba

YEAR-ROUND
SUMMER
MIGRATION

Size: 36–40" (91–102 cm); up to 4½' wingspan

Male: Tall, thin, all-white bird with a long neck and a long, pointed yellow bill. Black, stilt-like legs and black feet.

Female: same as male

Juvenile: same as adults

Nest: platform; male and female construct; 1 brood per year

Eggs: 2–3; light blue without markings

Incubation: 23–26 days; female and male incubate

Fledging: 43–49 days; female and male feed the young

Migration: non-migrator in eastern Texas

Food: small fish, aquatic insects, frogs, crayfish

Compare: Cattle Egret (p. 397) is about half the size of Great Egret and has a much shorter neck and much smaller bill. The Snowy Egret (p. 401) is much smaller, with yellow feet and a black bill. Juvenile Little Blue Heron (p. 127) is smaller and has a black-tipped gray bill. White Ibis (p. 403) has a very long, down-curved orange-to-red bill.

Stan's Notes: Slowly stalks shallow ponds, lakes and wetlands in search of small fish to spear with its long, sharp bill. Gives a loud, dry croak if disturbed or when squabbling for a nest site at the colony. The name "Egret" comes from the French word *aigrette,* meaning "ornamental tufts of plumes." The plumes grow near the tail during the breeding season. Hunted to near extinction in the 1800s and early 1900s for its long plumes, which were used to decorate women's hats. Today, the egret is a protected species.

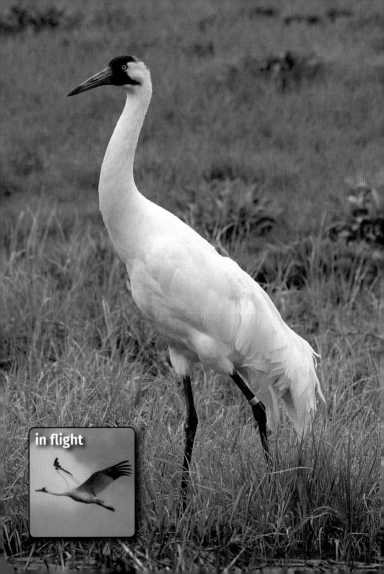

in flight

MIGRATION
WINTER

Whooping Crane
Grus americana

Size: 51–53" (130–135 cm); up to 7¼' wingspan

Male: White bird with a distinctive red crown and red patch just behind the bill (malar mark). Long dark legs. A long, pointed yellow bill. Black wing tips, seen in flight.

Female: same as male

Juvenile: similar to adult, tan to cinnamon brown, turns white during first winter

Nest: ground; female and male construct; 1 brood per year

Eggs: 1–3; cream to white with brown markings

Incubation: 29–31 days; female and male incubate

Fledging: 80–90 days; female and male feed young

Migration: complete to coastal Texas

Food: insects, fruit, fish, small mammals, seeds

Compare: Sandhill Crane (p. 349) is gray and lacks the malar mark. American White Pelican (p. 411) is smaller and holds head near body in flight.

Stan's Notes: The tallest bird in North America, but it weighs only 10–15 pounds (5–7 kg). The Whooper is the rarest of 15 crane species worldwide and one of only two native to North America. An endangered crane with only 15 birds remaining in 1949. Almost always in marshy habitats in family groups of three or more. Can fly up to 50 miles (80 km) per hour. Takes off by running into wind with wings outstretched. Wingspan equal to or slightly larger than Bald Eagle. Matures at 4–6 years and can live 25 years or more. Thought to mate for life. Mated pairs defend territory of 30–50 acres (12–20 ha). Migrates to northern Canada to nest and raise young.

breeding

in flight

chick-feeding
adult

American White Pelican

Pelecanus erythrorhynchos

YEAR-ROUND
MIGRATION

Size: 60–64" (152–163 cm); up to 9' wingspan

Male: Large white pelican with an enormous bright-yellow-to-orange bill. Yellow legs and feet. Black wing tips and trailing edge of wings. Breeding plumage has a bright-orange bill, legs and feet. Chick-feeding adult (an adult that is feeding young) has a gray-black crown.

Female: same as male

Juvenile: duller white than adult, with a brownish head and neck

Nest: ground, scraped-out depression rimmed with dirt; female and male build; 1 brood per year

Eggs: 1–3; white without markings

Incubation: 29–36 days; male and female incubate

Fledging: 60–70 days; female and male feed the young

Migration: complete to non-migrator in Texas

Food: fish

Compare: Brown Pelican (p. 273) has a gray-brown body and a black belly. Look for American White Pelican's black wing tips in flight.

Stan's Notes: Often seen in large groups on the larger lakes and reservoirs of Texas. Doesn't dive to catch fish, like coastal Brown Pelicans. Instead, groups swim and dip their bills simultaneously into water to scoop up fish. Groups fly in a large V, often gliding, followed by simultaneous flapping. Large flocks swirl on columns of rising warm air (thermals) on hot days. Breeding adults typically grow a flat, fibrous plate on the upper bill, which drops off after the eggs hatch. Usually silent; gives short grunts at the nesting colony.

male

female

Lesser Goldfinch
Spinus psaltria

YEAR-ROUND

Size: 4½" (11 cm)

Male: Striking bright yellow beneath from chin to base of tail. Black head, tail and wings. White patches on wings. Eastern variety has a black back. Western has a green back.

Female: dull yellow underneath, lacks a black head and back

Juvenile: same as female

Nest: cup; female builds; 1–2 broods per year

Eggs: 4–5; pale blue without markings

Incubation: 10–12 days; female incubates

Fledging: 12–14 days; female and male feed young

Migration: partial migrator to non-migrator; will move around the state to find food

Food: seeds, insects; will come to seed feeders

Compare: The male American Goldfinch (p. 415) is slightly larger and has a yellow back, unlike the black back of male Lesser Goldfinch.

Stan's Notes: There are two varieties of Lesser Goldfinch. Eastern males, with black backs, can be found in eastern and southern Texas, with western males, with green backs, to the north and west. Some females are extremely pale. Prefers forest edges or places with short trees and a consistent water source. Unlike many other birds, its diet is about 96 percent seed, even during peak insect season. Will come to seed feeders. Late summer nesters. Male feeds the incubating female by regurgitating partially digested seeds. Pairs stay together all winter. Winter flocks can number in the hundreds.

male

winter male

female

American Goldfinch
Spinus tristis

WINTER

Size: 5" (13 cm)

Male: Canary-yellow finch with a black forehead and tail. Black wings with white wing bars. White rump. No markings on the chest. Winter male is similar to the female.

Female: dull olive-yellow plumage with brown wings; lacks a black forehead

Juvenile: same as female

Nest: cup; female builds; 1 brood per year

Eggs: 4–6; pale blue without markings

Incubation: 10–12 days; female incubates

Fledging: 11–17 days; female and male feed the young

Migration: non-migrator to partial migrator; small flocks of up to 20 birds move around to find food

Food: seeds, insects; will come to seed feeders

Compare: The male Lesser Goldfinch (p. 413) has a black back. The Pine Siskin (p. 135) and female House Finch (p. 137) both have a streaked chest. The male Wilson's Warbler (p. 417) lacks black wings.

Stan's Notes: A common backyard resident. Most often found in open fields, scrubby areas and woodlands. Enjoys Nyjer seed in feeders. Lines its nest with the silky down from wild thistle. Almost always in small flocks. Twitters while it flies. Flight is roller coaster-like. Often called Wild Canary due to the male's canary-colored plumage. Male sings a pleasant, high-pitched song.

female

male

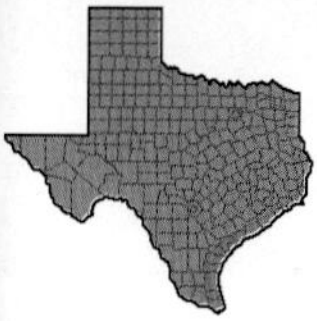

Wilson's Warbler

Cardellina pusilla

MIGRATION
WINTER

Size: 4¾" (12 cm)

Male: Dull-yellow upper and bright-yellow lower. Distinctive black cap. Large black eyes and small thin bill.

Female: same as male, but lacking the black cap

Juvenile: similar to female

Nest: cup; female builds; 1 brood per year

Eggs: 4–6; white with brown markings

Incubation: 10–13 days; female incubates

Fledging: 8–11 days; female and male feed young

Migration: complete, to coastal Texas

Food: insects

Compare: Male American Goldfinch (p. 415) has a black forehead and black wings. The male Common Yellowthroat (p. 419) has a very distinctive black mask.

Stan's Notes: A widespread warbler seen during migration and in winter. Can be found near water in willow and alder thickets. Its all-insect diet makes it one of the top insect-eating birds in North America. Often flicks its tail and spreads its wings when hopping among thick shrubs, looking for insects. Females often mate with males that have the best territories and that might already have mates (polygyny).

male

female

Common Yellowthroat

Geothlypis trichas

YEAR-ROUND
SUMMER
MIGRATION
WINTER

Size: 5" (13 cm)

Male: Olive-brown with a bright-yellow throat and chest, a white belly and a distinctive black mask outlined in white. Long, thin, pointed black bill.

Female: similar to male but lacks a black mask

Juvenile: same as female

Nest: cup; female builds; 2 broods per year

Eggs: 3–5; white with brown markings

Incubation: 11–12 days; female incubates

Fledging: 10–11 days; female and male feed the young

Migration: complete to non-migrator in Texas

Food: insects

Compare: The male American Goldfinch (p. 415) has a black forehead and wings. The Yellow-rumped Warbler (p. 287) only has patches of yellow and lacks the yellow chest of the Yellowthroat. Male Wilson's Warbler (p. 417) lacks the male Yellowthroat's black mask.

Stan's Notes: A common warbler of open fields and marshes. Sings a cheerful, well-known "witchity-witchity-witchity-witchity" song from deep within tall grasses. Male sings from prominent perches and while he hunts. He performs a curious courtship display, bouncing in and out of tall grass while singing a mating song. Female builds a nest low to the ground. Young remain dependent on their parents longer than most other warblers. A frequent cowbird host. Becomes more abundant in winter when northern birds migrate to Texas. Usually quiet and secretive during winter.

Orange-crowned Warbler
Oreothlypis celata

SUMMER
MIGRATION
WINTER

Size: 5" (13 cm)

Male: An overall pale-yellow bird with a dark line through eyes. Faint streaking on sides and chest. Tawny orange crown, often invisible. Small thin bill.

Female: same as male, but very slightly duller, often indistinguishable in the field

Juvenile: same as adults

Nest: cup; female builds; 1–2 broods per year

Eggs: 3–6; white with brown markings

Incubation: 12–14 days; female incubates

Fledging: 8–10 days; female and male feed young

Migration: complete, to Texas, Mexico and Central America

Food: insects, fruit, nectar

Compare: Male Common Yellowthroat (p. 419) has a distinctive black mask. Wilson's Warbler (p. 417) is brighter yellow with a distinct black cap.

Stan's Notes: This bird is often seen more during migration when large groups move together. Builds a bulky, well-concealed nest on the ground with nest rim at ground level. Known to drink flower nectar. The orange crown tends to be hidden and is rarely seen in the field. A widespread breeder, from western Texas to Alaska and across Canada and south to California.

Pine Warbler
Setophaga pinus

YEAR-ROUND
WINTER

Size: 5½" (14 cm)

Male: A yellow throat and breast with faint black streaks on sides of breast. Olive-green back. Two white wing bars. White belly.

Female: similar to male, only paler

Juvenile: similar to adults, but is browner with more white on belly

Nest: cup; female builds; 2–3 broods per year

Eggs: 3–5; white with brown markings

Incubation: 10–12 days; female incubates

Fledging: 12–14 days; female and male feed the young

Migration: non-migrator to partial migrator in Texas

Food: insects, seeds, fruit

Compare: The Yellow-rumped Warbler (p. 287) has yellow patches on its rump. Similar size as the American Goldfinch (p. 415) which lacks streaks on the breast.

Stan's Notes: A very common year-round resident of pine forests in the eastern half of the state. Nests only in pine forest. Brighter in spring and more drab in fall, it varies in color depending upon the time of year. Thought to have a larger bill than the other warblers. Sometimes is easier to identify by its song than by sight. Listen for a twittering, musical song that varies in speed.

male

female

Dickcissel
Spiza americana

Size: 6" (15 cm)

Male: A small thick-billed bird with yellow chest, belly and eyebrows. A distinctive black bib under a white chin. Chestnut wings.

Female: same as male, but lacking the black bib

Juvenile: similar to female, only duller overall

Nest: cup, made of plant stems, grass and leaves; female builds; 1 brood per year

Eggs: 4–6; pale blue without markings

Incubation: 12–13 days; female incubates

Fledging: 9–11 days; female feeds young

Migration: complete, to Mexico, Central America and South America

Food: insects, seeds

Compare: The Western Meadowlark (p. 439) is larger and has a prominent black V-shaped necklace unlike the Dickcissel's black bib.

Stan's Notes: Originally a bird of the prairie, now found in alfalfa fields, abandoned fields and meadows due to the loss of native prairie habitat. Prefers habitat that is sparsely vegetative. Doesn't do well in thick, dense vegetation. The males arrive at breeding sites a couple weeks before the females and begin to sing from prominent perches. Often seen singing from a fence post because it's the tallest object around. Nest is bulky, only a couple feet above ground and usually well concealed. Common name comes from an imitation of its song.

male
p. 371

female

SUMMER
MIGRATION

Baltimore Oriole
Icterus galbula

Size: 7–8" (18–20 cm)

Female: Pale yellow with orange tones and gray-brown wings with white wing bars. Gray bill. Dark eyes.

Male: flaming orange with a black head and back, white-and-orange wing bars, an orange-and-black tail, a gray bill and dark eyes

Juvenile: same as female

Nest: pendulous; female builds; 1 brood per year

Eggs: 4–5; bluish with brown markings

Incubation: 12–14 days; female incubates

Fledging: 12–14 days; female and male feed the young

Migration: complete, to Mexico, Central America and South America

Food: insects, fruit, nectar; comes to nectar, orange-half and grape-jelly feeders

Compare: The female Orchard Oriole (p. 429) has a dull-yellow belly. Look for the gray-brown wings to identify the female Baltimore Oriole.

Stan's Notes: A fantastic songster, often heard before seen. Easily attracted to bird feeders that offer sugar water (nectar), orange halves or grape jelly. Parents bring young to feeders. Sits at the top of trees, feeding on caterpillars. Female builds a sock-like nest at the outermost branches of tall trees. Prefers parks, yards and forests and often returns to the same area year after year. Some of the last birds to arrive in spring (April to May) and first to leave in fall (September).

male
p. 373

female

first-year
male

Orchard Oriole
Icterus spurius

SUMMER

Size: 7–8" (18–20 cm)

Female: Olive-green with a dull-yellow belly. Gray wings with 2 indistinct white wing bars. Long, thin bill with a gray mark on the lower bill.

Male: dark orange with black head, throat, upper back, wings and tail; 1 white wing bar

Juvenile: same as female; first-year male looks like the female, with a black bib

Nest: pendulous; female builds; 1 brood per year

Eggs: 3–5; pale blue to white, brown markings

Incubation: 11–12 days; female and male incubate

Fledging: 11–14 days; female and male feed the young

Migration: complete, to Mexico, Central America and northern South America

Food: insects, fruit, nectar; comes to nectar, orange-half and grape-jelly feeders

Compare: Female Baltimore Oriole (p. 427) is similar, but has orange tones and more-distinct wing bars. The female Summer Tanager (p. 433) is mustard-yellow with a larger bill.

Stan's Notes: Named "Orchard" for its preference for orchards. Also likes open woods. Eats insects until wild fruit starts to ripen. One of the last birds to arrive in spring and one of the first to leave in fall. Spends 4–5 months in Texas. Often nests alone; sometimes nests in small colonies. Parents bring their young to bird feeding stations after they fledge. Many people don't see these birds at feeders much during the summer and think they have left, but the birds are still there, hunting for insects to feed to their young. Often migrates in flocks with Baltimore Orioles.

male
p. 375

female

Bullock's Oriole
Icterus bullockii

SUMMER

Size: 8" (20 cm)

Female: Dull-yellow head and chest. Gray-to-black wings with white wing bars. A pale-white belly. Gray back, as seen in flight.

Male: bright-orange-and-black bird with a bold white patch on wings

Juvenile: similar to female

Nest: pendulous; female and male build; 1 brood per year

Eggs: 4–6; pale white to gray, brown markings

Incubation: 12–14 days; female incubates

Fledging: 12–14 days; female and male feed young

Migration: complete, to Mexico and Central America

Food: insects, berries, nectar; visits nectar feeders

Compare: Female Baltimore Oriole (p. 427) has a gray-brown back and wings. The female Scott's Oriole (p. 435) is larger and lacks the pale-white belly. Look for the female Bullock's dull-yellow and gray appearance.

Stan's Notes: So closely related to Baltimore Orioles of the eastern U.S., at one time both were considered a single species. Interbreeds with Baltimores where their ranges overlap. Most common in the state where cottonwood trees grow along rivers and other wetlands. Also found at edges of clearings, in city parks, on farms and along irrigation ditches. Hanging sock-like nest is constructed of plant fibers such as inner bark of junipers and willows. Will incorporate yarn and thread into its nest if offered at the time of nest building.

male
p. 383

female

Summer Tanager
Piranga rubra

SUMMER

Size: 8" (20 cm)

Female: Some show a faint wash of red, but most females are a mustard-yellow overall with slightly darker wings.

Male: bright rosy-red bird with darker red wings

Juvenile: male has patches of red and green over the entire body, female is same as adult female

Nest: cup; female builds; 1–2 broods per year

Eggs: 3–5; pale blue with dark markings

Incubation: 10–12 days; female incubates

Fledging: 12–15 days; female and male feed young

Migration: complete, to Central and South America

Food: insects, fruit

Compare: Female Orchard Oriole (p. 429) and Baltimore Oriole (p. 427) are similar, but they have wing bars. Look for Summer Tanager's lack of wing bars and larger, thicker bill to identify.

Stan's Notes: Found in Texas where woodlands exist, especially in mixed pine and oak forests. Due to clearing of land for agriculture, populations have decreased for over a century and especially most recently. Returning to Texas in late April and with young hatching in late May, some pairs have two broods per year. While fruit makes up some of the diet, most of it consists of insects such as bees and wasps. Summer Tanagers unfortunately seem to be parasitized by Brown-headed Cowbirds.

433

male

female

Scott's Oriole
Icterus parisorum

SUMMER

Size: 9" (22.5 cm)

Male: Black head, neck, back, upper breast and tail. Lemon-yellow belly, shoulders and rump. Long, pointed, slightly down-curved black bill. Dark eyes. Two white wing bars.

Female: similar to male, but has much less black

Juvenile: grayer than female, yellow under belly only

Nest: pendulous; female builds; 1–2 broods a year

Eggs: 2–4; pale blue with brown markings

Incubation: 14–16 days; female and male incubate

Fledging: 14–16 days; female and male feed young

Migration: complete, to Mexico

Food: insects, fruit, nectar; will come to orange or grapefruit halves and nectar feeders

Compare: The female Bullock's Oriole (p. 431) has a pale-white belly. Male American Goldfinch (p. 415) is much smaller and has black on the forehead, not on the entire head.

Stan's Notes: Found in open dry areas often associated with yucca and palm. Like other oriole species, female constructs a sock-like pouch that hangs from the end of a thin branch or is woven into a hole in a palm leaf. Populations have increased over the past 100 years due to planting of palm trees. Male is yellow, not orange, like other male orioles. Hunts by gleaning insects and caterpillars from leaves. Uses its long pointed bill to poke holes in bases of flowers to get nectar. Parents feed their young by regurgitating a mixture of insects and fruit. Named after General Winfield Scott, who fought in the Mexican War.

Western Kingbird
Tyrannus verticalis

SUMMER

Size: 9" (22.5 cm)

Male: Bright-yellow belly and yellow under wings. Gray head and chest, often with white chin. Wings and tail are dark gray to nearly black with white outer edges on tail.

Female: same as male

Juvenile: similar to adult, less yellow and more gray

Nest: cup; female and male construct; 1 brood per year

Eggs: 3–4; white with brown markings

Incubation: 18–20 days; female incubates

Fledging: 16–18 days; female and male feed young

Migration: complete, to Central America

Food: insects, berries

Compare: The Eastern Kingbird (p. 303) lacks any yellow of the Western Kingbird. The Great Kiskadee (p. 441) shares the yellow belly, but has a black-and-white head pattern. Western Meadowlark (p. 439) also shares the yellow belly of Western Kingbird, but it has a distinctive black V-shaped necklace.

Stan's Notes: A bird of open country, frequently seen sitting on top of the same shrub or fence post. Hunts by watching for crickets, bees, grasshoppers and other insects and flying out to catch them, then returns to perch. Parents teach young how to hunt, bringing wounded insects back to the nest for the young to chase. Returns in March. Builds nest in April, often in a fork of a small single trunk tree. Nests in trees around farms and homesteads.

Eastern
Meadowlark

Western Meadowlark
Sturnella neglecta

YEAR-ROUND
WINTER

Size: 9" (22.5 cm)

Male: Heavy-bodied bird with a short tail. Yellow chest and brown back. Prominent V-shaped black necklace. White outer tail feathers.

Female: same as male

Juvenile: same as adult

Nest: cup, on the ground in dense cover; female builds; 2 broods per year

Eggs: 3–5; white with brown markings

Incubation: 13–15 days; female incubates

Fledging: 11–13 days; female and male feed young

Migration: non-migrator to partial migrator

Food: insects, seeds

Compare: Western Kingbird (p. 437) shares the yellow belly, but it lacks the V-shaped black necklace. Horned Lark (p. 169) lacks the yellow chest and belly. Look for a black V marking on the chest to help identify the Meadowlark.

Stan's Notes: Named "Meadowlark" because it's a bird of meadows and sings like the larks of Europe. Best known for its wonderful song—a flute-like, clear whistle. Often seen perching on fence posts but quickly dives into tall grass when approached. Conspicuous white marks on sides of tail, seen when flying away. Not in the lark family; a blackbird family member and is related to grackles and orioles. Overall population is down greatly due to agricultural activities and ditch mowing. Ranges of Eastern and Western Meadowlarks overlap in the state (map reflects the combined range). The birds are hard to distinguish, but Western is paler yellow and grayer than Eastern and sings a different song.

YEAR-ROUND

Great Kiskadee
Pitangus sulphuratus

Size: 10" (25 cm)

Male: A handsome flycatcher. Bright sulfur-yellow chest and belly with a bold black-and-white striped head. White chin and throat. Dull reddish-brown back, wings and tail. Yellow crown patch is concealed.

Female: same as male

Juvenile: similar to adult, but not as brightly colored

Nest: modified cup, ball-shaped, covered; female and male build; 1–2 broods per year

Eggs: 3–6; pale white to cream with brown marks

Incubation: 13–15 days; female incubates

Fledging: 15–20 days; female and male feed young

Migration: non-migrator; moves around to find food

Food: insects, berries, small fish

Compare: Larger than Western Kingbird (p. 437), which shares a yellow belly but lacks the bold black-and-white head pattern.

Stan's Notes: Brightly colored flycatcher, unlike most others. Seen in densely vegetated areas and brushy woods near water. Sits in the open, sunning itself and drying out after diving in water for aquatic insects and small fish, which is uncommon in flycatchers. Waits on a perch, watching for passing insects, then flies out to snatch one and returns to the same perch. Often beats prey against a branch several times to stun or kill it before eating. Will usually chase away other birds that enter its territory. Named for its loud, screaming "kiss-ka-dee" call. Also gives a loud "sree-ah." Range is restricted to southern Texas in the U.S., but extends into Central America.

BIRDING ON THE INTERNET

Birding online is a great way to discover additional information and learn more about birds. These websites will assist you in your pursuit of birds. Web addresses sometimes change a bit, so if one no longer works, just enter the name of the group into a search engine to track down the new address.

Site	Address
Author Stan Tekiela's homepage	naturesmart.com
American Birding Association	aba.org
Audubon Texas	tx.audubon.org
Blackland Prairie Raptor Center	bpraptorcenter.org
The Cornell Lab of Ornithology	birds.cornell.edu
eBird	ebird.org
Houston Audubon	houstonaudubon.org
Texas Ornithological Society	texasbirds.org
Wildlife Rescue & Rehabilitation	wildlife-rescue.org

CHECKLIST/INDEX BY SPECIES

Use the boxes to check the birds you've seen.

MORE FOR TEXAS BY STAN TEKIELA

Identification Guides

Birds of Prey of the South
Field Guide

Cactus of Texas Field Guide

The Kids' Guide to Birds of Texas

Mammals of Texas Field Guide

Trees of Texas Field Guide

Wildflowers of Texas Field Guide

Nature Books

Bird Trivia

Start Mushrooming

A Year in Nature with Stan Tekiela

Children's Books:
Adventure Board Book Series

Floppers & Loppers

Paws & Claws

Peepers & Peekers

Snouts & Sniffers

Children's Books

C is for Cardinal

Can You Count the Critters?

Critter Litter

Critter Litter Southwest

Children's Books:
Wildlife Picture Books

Baby Bear Discovers the World

The Cutest Critter

Do Beavers Need Blankets?

Hidden Critters

Jump, Little Wood Ducks

Some Babies Are Wild

Super Animal Powers

What Eats That?

Whose Baby Butt?

Whose Butt?

Whose Track Is That?

Wildlife Appreciation Series
Amazing Hummingbirds
Backyard Birds
Bears
Bird Migration
Cranes, Herons & Egrets
Deer, Elk & Moose
Fascinating Loons
Intriguing Owls
Wild Birds

Nature Appreciation Series
Bird Nests
Feathers
Wildflowers

Our Love of Wildlife Series
Our Love of Hummingbirds
Our Love of Loons
Our Love of Owls

Adventure Quick Guides
Birds of the South
Birds of the Southwest
Shorebirds of the Southeast & Gulf States

Nature's Wild Cards (playing cards)
Bears
Birds of the Southwest/Gulf
Hummingbirds
Loons
Mammals of the Southwest/Gulf
Owls
Raptors
Trees of the Southwest/Gulf
Wildflowers of the Gulf

ABOUT THE AUTHOR

Naturalist, wildlife photographer and writer Stan Tekiela is the originator of the popular state-specific field guide series that includes the *Wildflowers of Texas Field Guide*. Stan has authored more than 190 educational books, including field guides, quick guides, nature books, children's books, and more, presenting many species of animals and plants.

With a Bachelor of Science degree in natural history from the University of Minnesota and as an active professional naturalist for more than 30 years, Stan studies and photographs wildlife throughout the United States and Canada. He has received national and regional awards for his books and photographs and is also a well-known columnist and radio personality. His syndicated column appears in more than 25 newspapers, and his wildlife programs are broadcast on a number of Midwest radio stations. Stan can be contacted via his website, at naturesmart.com.